Baba Is Here

Conversations with God on His Omnipresence

Graciela Busto

Translated by Anthony Albanese

L EELA PRESS INC.
A Non-Profit Corporation
Faber, VA

English edition first published in 1998 by
Leela Press, Inc.
4026 River Road
Faber, VA 22938

Translated from Spanish by Anthony Albanese
Baba Está Aquí by Graciela Busto
© 1992 Errepar, S.A., Buenos Aires, Italy

English Edition, First printing, June 1998
© 1997 Leela Press, Inc.

Library of Congress Catalog No. 97-076043
Baba Is Here: conversations with God on His omnipresence/
written by Graciela Busto

ISBN 1-887906-01-0

TABLE OF CONTENTS

FOREWORD

Graciela Busto's conversation with her inner voice as expressed in her book *Baba is Here, Conversations with God on His Omnipresence,* is a beautiful example of how we can find remarkable guidance by turning within. This piece of illuminated writing is special, as most of us do not find inner guidance in such a clear and articulate way. There is much to gain from this writing, as it holds such a strong and rich ring of Sai Baba's teachings and can inspire us, help us find direction, and give us confidence that when we turn inside, we too can have such a potent experience of the Lord's omnipresence.

As we read and digest these words, however, there is an element of caution we should exercise. Because Swami has told us that there is no intermediary between Himself and each of us, and because we must not mistake anyone as a medium or a special conduit through which Swami speaks, it is important to put the writing in a certain perspective. Swami, telling us that He is omnipresent and that we can make contact with Him inside, does not mean that promptings from inside are clear and direct emanations from Him to be followed with full faith. When we feel His promptings, it is our responsibility to use discrimination and reason in evaluating the truth of them and their meaning to us, as there can be some distortion as they move through the personality. No matter how enlightened a piece may seem, we should understand this limitation. Although we can gain greatly from inspired and elevated writings, it is not the same as studying and digesting Swami's direct, pure words in which we can place full faith.

With this in mind, there is so much to be gained from this particular writing as it brings us so close to Swami's heart. And it encourages us to turn inward, listen for Swami's direction and to sharpen our discrimination. This experience of turning inward with discrimination will no doubt bring us swiftly to Swami's lotus feet

Leela Press

Translator's Note

First, I would like to thank Graciela Busto for her beautiful book, which has touched me so deeply.

I would like also to offer my heartfelt thanks to Daniel Coifman, Marya Kivistik, *Leela Press,* and all who helped improve this translation with their editing corrections. I would like to thank Lola Goldberg for copyediting the manuscript.

I offer my gratitude and love to my wife, Adorine, for her patience and support throughout the years, and especially during the time I was translating *Baba is Here.*

This translation is dedicated with love and placed at the divine lotus feet of Bhagavan Sri Sathya Sai Baba. This work is the result of His inspiration and blessings.

Om Sai Ram
A. P. Albanese

PREFACE

This book records a series of inner conversations I had with Sai Baba on God's omnipresence. It is because He is omnipresent that I have been able to receive inner messages from Him. He is always everywhere, in our homes, our hearts, and in our minds.

I want to make it very clear that I am not in any way special in being able to receive these messages. Swami has frequently said your own inner voice is Me speaking to you. Because of the Lord's omnipresence, all people can have access to direct inner communication with Him. In the book, when I quote the words of Sai Baba in answer to questions that I have posed, the response is coming from my inner voice. These words are not and should not be quoted as coming directly from Bhagavan Sathya Sai Baba.

Also included are inner dialogues with Swami on subjects such as pride, forgiveness, and free will. My inner conversations with Baba are as real as if I were talking to Him in the interview room.

When I first received these divine messages, I was uncertain as to whether they really came from Baba. Was it really Swami speaking? I wasn't sure. When I presented the manuscript of my first book to him in Prasanthi Nilayam, I asked if the messages were really from Him. He responded in a strong voice, "Without a doubt!" and He signed the manuscript. I rejoiced in this confirmation from the Lord.

Leela Press had similar concerns about publishing the English translation of *Baba is Here.* They felt they could not go ahead without Swami's verbal approval. Fortunately, a member of their family was on her way to Prasanthi Nilayam and took the manuscript with her. During an interview, she offered the manuscript to Swami, saying, *"Leela Press* wants to publish this book. They need Your specific permission because the book consists of conversations with You that were not received in person, but were received as inner messages." To be sure she was making herself clear, she repeated the statement twice.

Swami took the manuscript, looked through the pages, and approvingly said, "Yes, good, and signed it, "With Love, Baba." It was thrilling for me to again receive confirmation directly from the Lord that these teachings are coming from Him.

At the feet of Baba, G.B.

PROLOGUE

Baba's Message to Me

"Gold shines in the depths of the undiscovered vein even though the deposit has not yet been discovered. In the same way, the divine spark shines in your heart, even when the darkness of ignorance covers the untold riches existing within you.

"To dive into the depths of your being requires daring and an adventuresome spirit; it requires periods of fruitless searching and exhaustion. But when you finally find the limitless vein of spiritual truth, you become the owner of the greatest treasure conceivable.

"All of you have a gold vein within you that you have not yet discovered. Spiritual discipline is the tool needed to penetrate the rock of delusion, so that you will find the vein of gold that eliminates all your doubts, fears, and self-rejection.

"Repeating that God is immanent is not enough to realize this truth; it is not even sufficient when the Lord Himself tells this to you. You must experience it directly in the depths of your inner self where the precious metal of transcendental knowledge shines.

"You cannot advance while remaining motionless. Take My hand and walk with Me. Open yourself to the reality of My presence. I am the driver. I am the One who knows. I am the One who commands. I am the One who understands. I am the One who sees in the darkness and reveals to you the Self, the immortal treasure that awaits your discovery.

"When you allow Me to point you in the right direction, the gold of divine love will shine in your life and enrich you beyond measure."

PART ONE

Divine Omnipresence

Forms of Divine Omnipresence

"Swami, in how many ways does omnipresence manifest?"

"In three ways. In the first you say: 'Look, the Lord is here!' You see Him in front of you, tangible, describable. You see him with your eyes, even though your reason indicates that it is impossible that the Lord is actually here. Yet, He is here, because the Lord's form can be perceived in many places at once.

"The second form of omnipresence is when you become aware afterward that the Lord was with you. If He says: 'I saw you when you were doing this or that,' 'I heard you telling that story,' 'I know what you did,' He is confirming His presence, which you were not aware of at that time. This is showing you that He is omnipresent. In the first example, you see the Lord; in the second example, He tells you, 'I know because I was with you.'"

"And Swami, what about the third way?"

"The third way refers to the direct participation of the Lord in your daily life. His intervention becomes evident to you because of how your affairs develop. You see apparently insurmountable problems resolve themselves: Either you come out of an accident uninjured or, when the Lord appears by virtue of His power, you know He has helped you, and this strong certainty makes you affirm, 'It was my Master who was here and did this.'"

Manifestation

"It happened during my vacation. There was a tremendous commotion in the house. We were all quarreling. There seemed to be unresolvable differences between everyone. I had the feeling that our anxiously awaited holiday of rest and recreation would be a big failure.

"I decided to leave the scene and walked to the nearby beach; I was upset and feeling sad and lonely. Thinking of Baba, I sat at the edge of the water. Almost without realizing what I was doing, I began to sing bhajans (devotional songs). The songs to the Lord were coming effortlessly, one after the other. I was singing aloud and my heart was becoming peaceful, happy, and full of hope. I then asked Swami to grace us with unity, friendship and harmony. I asked Him to allow us to share these days just as we had planned them. Then I continued singing.

"Suddenly, looking deeply into the water and the afternoon sky, already a deep blue, I noticed that the sky's reflection on the water had dramatically changed; now the sea was coming to me with an orange glow, the foam was orange at the edge, and the receding water was leaving an orange glitter on the sand. I knew that Baba was present. Deeply moved, I continued to sing to Him, knowing that this was my way to elevate my prayer to the Supreme.

"After an absence of two hours, I returned to the house. There I found everyone in harmony. There were no more problems. The Lord had taken charge."

(As told by a devotee at the Uriarte Center
in Buenos Aires, Argentina, on February 1, 1991.)

Surrender

"It is not enough that you become conscious of My presence within you; you must also realize that this presence is all powerful.

"Become sensitive to God's powerful presence. It is only waiting for the opportunity to show itself. If you are conscious of this gift, you will not act on your own, but you will say, 'Baba, please, You act for me, You answer for me, You direct me.' Then your conduct will become perfect. There will be neither blame nor doubts, only devotion, peace, and contentment.

"Constantly practice this surrender. I will continue to teach this until it becomes second nature to you. You must only say, 'Swami, please do it for me.' You must let Me have the reins. When a devotee surrenders in this way, I give Myself to him completely without limit."

God's Time

"Swami, when it is stated that God is omnipresent, besides implying that God is everywhere simultaneously, does it also signify that only the present is God's time?"

"You say it well. For God there is no past nor future, only the present. That is why your errors are forgiven."

"I do not understand what you just said, Swami. What does it mean?"

"It means that, if you committed an error yesterday and you repent for that error today, God forgives you in the present for the error that occurred in the past. However, you would still be held accountable for any present error."

"But then, Swamiji, how can You explain that karma (action) produces consequences in a future life as a result of an action done in the past?"

"You must understand well the meaning of 'To God, everything is present.' When you throw a stone into a lake, you see waves resulting from the impact. You see them one after the other as they form in sequence, with the height of each wave being proportional to the distance from the impact. It is so, isn't it?"

"Yes, Lord."

"Now then, to God the impact and the formation of each

5

wave are simultaneous facts. He does not need to wait for the last wave to arrive at the shore to know its height or speed. The Lord knows in one instant, unique and present, all the past and all the future. When He is looking at you, He knows what has been and what will be in this and in other lives. That is why in Him there is neither haste nor reproach. The Lord adapts His conduct to your capacities and gives you the instruction necessary for your growth and evolution. He knows. Do not think that in permitting an act to be completed through the law of karma, which, in another life, appears as future to you, the Lord postpones or defers the settling of that karma. No. To God this is also in the present, for every moment is in the divine instant.

If there were past or future for the Supreme, you could then affirm that 'The Lord was.' But that is not possible. Such an affirmation would carry the possibility of 'not being,' and that is not possible for divinity. Nor can you speak of a future by saying, 'God will be.' This is a statement of a change in time, as if there were an instance—in this case, the present—in which God as yet is not. That is incompatible with His essence. God is always present. He is immutable, and He contains the whole universe.

"He is the seed, the tree, and its fruit simultaneously. But you cannot understand this. You see the mutable, the transitory. In your perception, you live as a result of what has already been—the memory—and what will come in the future. You have difficulty in establishing yourself in the unchanging present, which is God's time. As you progress toward Him, this will become more evident to your inner self. This present, illumined by His light and His presence, is where there is neither sorrow for the past nor anxiety for the future. There is only permanent serenity and joy.

"God sees your karma the instant an act is committed. Creation is unity, relative time is separation. I know what you think. You see your body and feel that whoever you were before you were born no longer exists. But, don't you feel in

6

the depths of your being that an unchanging awareness of self proclaims who you are, even when those who see you may say that you have changed? This identity is what is permanent in you. It is the only truth. It is the atma (your true Self), from which the spark of God illumines your awareness and reveals the truth of yourself that your Master is teaching you."

A Miracle in Spain

Dolores, an Argentinean devotee, tells us: "We were driving on a highway. In front of us a large truck, a tractor-trailer, was hauling flammable liquid in drums. It was late in the afternoon, and lights were beginning to be turned on. We were driving quite fast. Suddenly we saw the truck turning abruptly and the trailer turning over. The drums were catapulted in all directions. Many were furiously rolling toward our car. I covered my face with my hands and cried, 'Baba! Baba! Baba!' The noise, which the drums were making as they bounced around and about, was terrifying. I opened my eyes and was able to see that the drums were jumping and rolling by us without touching the car. They would come close to us—we had already stopped—and then would change direction, as if repelled by a magnetic force. None of the drums exploded, even though they were full. No one was able to believe we came out un-scathed. Later, everyone was commenting that it was Baba's miracle."

Divine Protection

"You must not fear the impact of any violence against you. No power may prevail against Mine. I am the guardian of My devotees. I decide their fate. When something difficult happens to you, think of Me and become conscious of My immediate help, even though you may not have any apparent indication of this help. I am in you, you are in Me, your protection is absolute. No matter what type of problem is confronting you, if you accept the peace that this certainty provides, your steps will take the right direction to find a quick and definitive solution. There is nothing impossible for your Master. Rest in My love and remember My words, 'Why fear when I am here?'"

Omnipresence and Faith

"Baba, Lord, is faith a necessary condition for the realization of the divine omnipresence?"

"Of course not. There are no conditions necessary to realize that God is present. Otherwise there would be no possible conversion caused by experience. Paul, on the road to Damascus, is a good example of this. He did not have faith in Christ, but His vision was an indisputable experience."

"Nevertheless, Swami, once you said that without faith it is not possible to achieve divine vision."

"When you are on the spiritual path, this is so. Doubt alters the perception of anything that transcends the five ordinary senses. Your intuition is blocked and your reasoning becomes incorrect; God becomes inaccessible to you. When you open your heart and clear yourself of doubts by surrendering to the Lord, not only do you see God, but you become aware that He was always there.

"There are circumstances in which the Lord's intervention prompts a dramatic transformation. The intensity of this transformation is in direct proportion to the degree of faith that becomes awakened in the person to whom the Lord directs His action. But, of course, these are very special cases."

"Baba, please, I still do not understand this. If I do not have faith in God, His being omnipresent has no value, for He is not omnipresent for me."

"Yes, He is. First, if God were not omnipresent, you could not exist. Second, negating God does not make His presence

8

less certain, nor does it make you unavailable to receive His gifts. From a purely practical viewpoint, you deny God because you do not know Him. This ignorance comes from false reasoning. It is the mind that denies; it is the ego, not the inner self. The inner self recognizes God in each object and vibrates with the divinity. Superficially, God does not exist for the atheist. But, in the atheist's intimate self, God waits for him to awaken and discover God as the only truth. What you propose is an old philosophical problem: Does the object exist without the observer who perceives it? Or, is existence independent of the knower? In the case of God, denial is the result of maya (the illusion of diversity), which hides the primary reality."

"Then, why Lord, at times, even though I know You to be omnipresent, do I still not find you?"

"There are two reasons. The first is because you close your heart to Me. The heart closes itself when you are too involved in the world. The heart closes when you let yourself be driven by opinions, expressions, conducts, and commentaries arising from human passions, as well as from a pessimistic, direct, down-to-earth sense about life. The heart closes itself when you interrupt your sadhana for reasons that do not coincide with God's. The heart closes itself when there is something you do not forgive, because you lose sight of the fact that I am everything.

"The second reason why you do not find Me, even though you know Me to be omnipresent, is because I hide Myself. Thus I offer you a chance to increase your faith, to search deeper inside yourself, to intensify your anguish and anxiety to find Me. This is God's play. If you know this, play and search for Me, for I only wish to be found."

A Chalice for the Lord

"Omnipresence can exist without faith, because God

9

existed before creation. God created faith in man's heart as a chalice wherein He may bestow His sweetness, which may thus quench man's thirst for eternity. Faith is a receptacle inside of you; empty it so that there may be a place for divine grace. Cast away your ego, your passions, your doubts, your fears, and your faults, and offer yourself as a chalice wherein I may pour My love."

Invoking God

"Swami, if God is omnipresent, why is it necessary to invoke Him?"

"God does not need your invocation. But, you need to invoke Him, because You do not realize His omnipresence; He is there, but you are not conscious of this; therefore you invoke Him so that you may be closer to Him, the Lord, who has responded before your call. By invoking God, you are calling upon your own faith. Although your faith may be hidden, you are calling upon the believer in yourself, so that you will attune yourself to the Supreme and recognize His presence."

"What happens if the Lord does not respond?"

"It is His way of prodding man to continue asking for His presence until he finds the proper call that will make God reveal Himself."

"Swami, doesn't God respond to every call?"

"Not in the way in which the one who calls expects it; God knows from where the human being is invoking Him; if it is from love, He will respond, regardless of what the person says. Many times devotees become confused. They curse, become angry, and whine, and, when they do so, they forsake love, supposing that in time they will create a space for God to manifest. But, this is not so. Tell the Lord what you prefer or want, but do not forsake love, because it is this powerful force that persuades Him to help you and give you solace. Love is the only invincible sentiment, the only way to tear the veil that impedes your finding Me present in you, and in everything, everywhere. There is no better way to invoke the Lord than to open your heart to love."

Swami, the Witness
Prasanthi Nilayam, January 1990

In our room, Cecilia and I were commenting about what happened at the last darshan.

"Did you see?" I said, "It looks as if Swami had no teeth; when He speaks you cannot see them."

"It's true," responded Cecilia, "I look at his mouth and I think that the entire universe fits inside."

During the next darshan, Cecilia and I were in the same row, next to each other. Baba passed by and stopped just a few steps away from us to exchange some words with a devotee. As He was doing so, he was looking at Cecilia and me with a broad smile on His face, allowing His teeth to show clearly. Sai Ram.

Other Subjects

The Words of the Lord

"The spiritual aspirant is never satisfied in his search for truth. God's words never seem redundant or too familiar. He always finds new meaning in them, even when he has already read or heard the truths of the Lord. That is why it is a mistake to attach less value to the words of the Master, just because you have previously read the same words in other writings. There are people who say, 'But I have already read this in the *Upanishads*! or 'Such and such guru has said the same thing before.' This repetition is natural. God does not contradict

11

Himself. In each era, He restates His teachings through different media, expressing them in different words. His message, which the true seeker can never totally decipher, is always the same.

"God's voice is infinite. He touches different chords of man's inner world, awakening emotions, intuitive awareness, and thoughts, which are personal for each individual. This is in accordance with each person's particular stage of evolution, his thirst for knowledge, and his surrender to the Supreme. Therefore, the inner voice is always new. The person who believes he knows the meaning of a lesson because he read it before is mistaken. God's voice does not repeat itself. It only resonates in an unending variety of ways in order to steer man toward the knowledge of unity, which is his destination.

"Surrender yourself to the voice of God and allow His principles to guide you, for they are ambrosia for the life of the spirit. Drink of the fountain that you have found in your Master, and take possession of His words as if they were yours; fix His thoughts in your heart, and become inebriated with His love. The reward will be Him, nothing less than God Himself."

Samadhi (I)

"Swami, how is it possible for man to write about samadhi, when during samadhi, he loses his perception of meditating and merges with the Absolute? He is living an experience that he is not conscious of until afterward. How could he write or speak about something that he did not perceive or know?"

"Man knows samadhi by how it affects him. No one who has reached this state can be the same afterward. Man knows that he was touched by the light because he awakens enlightened; his vision has become extraordinarily clear. His thought processes are very acute, and his detachment is perfect. No one can experience this transformation unless he has experienced samadhi, even if, as you say, he cannot remember it.

12

"In order for a man to be fully realized, he must pass through the state of non-being. This is the result of merging with the Absolute, the realization of the atma (the divine presence), in his inner self. Then he will recognize the One in whom there is no distinction between the knower, the known, and the process of knowing. In order to know something, that something must be separate from you, otherwise how could you know it? To know implies a time when you did not know, and this is impossible for the One who is All, who is always eternally self-aware. Therefore, it is not possible for Him to be conscious of a period when He is not aware. This is inconceivable to the Absolute.

"Consciousness of the change—before or after samadhi—is not inherent in the All. The All is changeless unity, the unknowable being in its pure state, the essence that is indivisible by instants of time, such as occurs in memory. Do you understand? Remembering is time-related, human. In the absolute present there is no remembering, there is only eternity. How can you freeze an experience in a time frame in order to recall it later on if, in the eternal, there is no movement, no time?

"You return here and try to evaluate the experience of samadhi. With what resources? Those that you possess in this dimension are insufficient; if the experience is indescribable, then why would you want to describe it? You are left with only a pale reflection of the experience. It is like awakening after a heavy rain; you know that it has rained because you see that the soil is wet. In reality you are supposing it has rained because the soil is wet. So, when man withdraws into meditation and then, coming out of that state, finds himself transformed, he then knows that he has passed through that dimension where he must have merged, if only for an instant, with the One. A profound certainty tells him that he was in a state of absolute bliss, just as when you forget a beautiful dream but are left with a nostalgic feeling that you have experienced something beautiful, even though you cannot remember it.

"Now you ask me, how was man able to write about this? Know that only great sages were able to lift the veil about this subject. It was divine grace that touched the spirit of those chosen ones, allowing their intellects to utter the words that would reveal what was secret. The divinity wanted it this way, in order to direct man to search his innermost self.

"Nevertheless, I must tell you something. Your questions express an almost exclusively rational vision. You believe that only when man separates himself from his experience can he understand it. But this is not so. Within the same experience is the knowledge of the experience. You do not need to reflect about it in order to know that it has happened, nor to say that you know about it and that you are conscious of what occurred. There is a way to know that is neither sequential nor logical. It is all encompassing, complete, and simultaneous. There are no steps, no reflection, no comprehension. This is knowledge in which what is known is one with the knower. Pure consciousness does not think, because there is no subject or object to think about. It is essence being itself. There is no reflection of the 'I' on itself; there is only complete perception of the truth, which is being truth itself. In this state, there is no process to obtain knowledge, there is only Being. Then you return to your regular life and, once again, time is sequential, again there is change, there is subject and object, you and the world.

"In that reality, where you are constrained by dimension and duality, you try to recreate the Absolute, to recover that instant of infinity, the eternity that was experienced. Then you want to say that the experience is not real, that perhaps the Master expressed Himself symbolically, or that you simply had a dream. You choose, by reasoning, to reject that blissful experience because you cannot understand it. That is why the Master has come; He is the road, the bridge, and the destination. Allow Him to guide you."

On Books and Reading

"All of the books you read appear to have contradictions in them. There is no contradiction in spiritual matters, only different viewpoints. They seem contradictory to you because you seek the absolute truth in each proposition, without realizing that there are stages, different levels, and, above all, the divine plan. What is written or said does not apply all of the time for everyone. Each person is given what is necessary in accordance with the stage reached. You have also passed through many stages, only you do not remember the stages you traversed before reaching Me.

"True masters are in harmony with the root of their teachings, with the marrow of their principles, with their essence. First you drink milk, then you eat baby food, then you stop eating it; if anyone suggests baby food you need not get confused, you know you have transcended this stage and realize this teaching is not for you. This teaching is given for others who need it.

"Swami sometimes addresses a large number of devotees in a manner that does not satisfy everyone. Many question why Baba says this or that, and then they feel uncomfortable or offended. They do not realize that My words are specifically meant for only some of those who are present. Only by speaking directly to them can I reach their consciousness during the meeting. Only then are they able to assimilate the teachings without feeling personally addressed. The public teachings of the Lord demand the humility and discrimination of each devotee. Always try to perceive a little beyond the apparent. Whether in books or in words, you will see that there is no contradiction in what God expounds; in Him there is only knowledge and love."

As Above So Below

"Swami, does the Law of Correspondence exist in all the different planes of manifestation? The principle of the Law states: 'As above so below'; does it mean that what is present in the divine is also present in the human?"

"The question you pose is a simplification. You cannot apply this principle to all the manifestations; perhaps you can do so with the human category. This axiom is given to man so that, by applying it, he may go beyond his passions and desires so that he may know how to orient himself in order to elevate his inclinations and character. But you cannot apply this law to the truth of God, because 'above' and 'below' indicate a relationship between opposites, and duality is not applicable in the realm of the divine. 'As above so below' is an axiom that the ancient masters proposed in order that the human being could sublimate that which is worldly and give his love to a superior entity. That is why God takes a human form. How could you otherwise conceive of Him, if not as human? Have you thought of this? There is no above or below in the Absolute, for there exists no comparison."

"Then, Baba, how can we apply this axiom in our lives?"

"You can apply it by learning to transmute. Listen carefully: transmutation implies change, transformation; this may have been your experience when I said to you, 'Take what is here, and put it there,' and thereby elevate it. For example: 'Use the energy that you generate in getting angry to forgive, employ the time you spend in getting depressed by using it for spiritual reading. Put what is here, there. What is worldly, direct toward what is lofty;' that is the ideal relationship in Hermes' axiom, to which you alluded. Apply it to the human dimension, the everyday plane of living. This constitutes a first step on the path of the spiritual aspirant who must learn to transcend each category in order to approach God."

"And yet, God appears so close..."

"If the Lord holds your hand, you see His hand as similar to yours, but would you affirm that His hand is equal to yours? The Lord approaches you, He tunes to your frequency so that you may vibrate in unison with Him. Then, little by little, He changes the vibratory rate in order to have you grow without much suffering, so that the impact of the change will not annihilate you. God brings you slowly from you to Him. However, do not think that because of the way in which He appears to you—those almost human aspects that you see—means that your Lord, God, is like you. God shows Himself to you in that manner in order for you to receive His teachings, which are uniquely exclusive for each devotee.

"I must tell you something: it is very good that you investigate ancient works and that you get to know the scriptures of the various religions, as well as the thoughts of the sages. But once the call of your Master has been uttered, you have to dedicate yourself to His teachings exclusively; He knows at what pace each truth may be poured into your intellect and which practice you must perform in each case. If you dedicate yourself to searching here and there, it will be inevitable that you will get confused; confusion moves you away from the voice of the Master; devotion then weakens, and you will not know anymore where you are headed. You will be full of knowledge, but you will not know why you have acquired it. Search where you were told the treasure lies hidden. Occupy your mind with the realization of the One without a second, follow My teachings and do not engage yourself in anything else."

Promises

"The offense to God does not consist in not having fulfilled a promise, but rather in having made it. First, because you cannot reward God. To say, 'If You give me this I will give You the other,' is to put a price on God's action, which is priceless. Second, making a promise to the Lord implies making a commitment about your future, to ensure the fulfillment of something that is beyond your decision. Your present conduct, as well as your future conduct, is determined by His will and not by yours. How then could you promise the fulfillment of an act in a time in which you have no certainty as to when it will be fulfilled? Third, you suppose He will punish you if you do not fulfill your promise. You are assigning your values to the Lord; He tells you that what you promise is your business and has nothing to do with God. You cannot tell God how to react when you fulfill or fail to fulfill a promise that you have made. No one can direct the will of God, nor can anyone say when God rewards or punishes; that is God's decision. Therefore, never promise anything to your Master. Just do what He tells you, nothing more."

God's Love (I)

"Swami, when I discover God within me, I love Him as something separate from me. When realizing that God is me, do I love myself? Likewise, when God loves the divinity inherent in my self, is He loving Himself?"

"That statement is incorrect. It is as if you were to ask me if the sun illumines itself. Let's begin with the second part of your question: God does not love giving love, God loves being. He is love. Each time you contact Him, you receive love, which is His essence, just as when you put yourself in the sun, you receive its light. It is not possible for the sun to negate its light, nor is it possible for the water not to wet, nor for the fire not to burn. Would you say that water wets itself? God's love is not

18

given as you give your affection to another person. In duality, there exists the possibility of direction, quality of sentiment, and the temporary nature of your love. You give something and another receives it. God does not give, God is. That is why you are told to put yourself in contact with Him, in order for you to enjoy His essence, which is clearly apparent and absolute. If God would give love, there would exist the possibility that He would not give it, choosing not to give something of Himself.

"It is not correct to ask if God loves Himself, because in your question a category is implied that is not applicable to Him. What is the Himself of God? Is it something outside of Him, something that can be separated? Do you want to know if He pours love upon Himself? To pour love upon Himself would signify incorporating something from outside into God. Then, what is the outside of God? In God, love is not a sentiment, it is an existence, an emanation, it is He Himself. You see, the light does not give itself. Light is. If you wish to enjoy light you have to approach it, and you will be illumined.

"Come near to God and you will receive His love, not because He gives it to you, but because you have come close to Him and you receive His emanation. Thus, God's love does not discriminate. It is received by anyone who approaches Him with an open heart. That is the only indispensable condition. If you claim it from afar and doubt that it is true, it will not happen, just as one who is in a cave with closed eyes cannot perceive light. If you desire to find the exit and grope in the dark with your eyes open, at some time you will see a glimmer. Run toward that glimmer, come out of the cave, and you will be bathed entirely in the light. So it is with the Supreme.

"God does not say, looking at His creatures, 'I love Myself,' just as love does not say, 'I love myself,' or the light say, 'I illumine myself.' God is a permanent effusion of love, which reaches all His manifestations; each human being is an 'embodiment of love'; He does not say, 'I love Me,' because who would be the 'Me' in that sentence?

"Now, as regards the first part of your question, the answer is: No, you do not love yourself when you find out that you are God, because the human being cannot transcend duality as long as he names something different from himself. That is why the enlightened person is not understood, because he speaks of something he alone understands; he has arrived beyond the perception of maya. He speaks of something that is inconceivable. You speak of your higher Self, God, but, simultaneously, you speak to Him and speak of Him; duality is there. You do not give love to yourself, you give it to God, to Him, to the One who dwells in you."

The Nature of Order

"Children are taught to be orderly from early childhood. Then in school this subject is impressed upon the child; when the teacher says, 'This student is orderly, he keeps his desk well organized,' this constitutes praise. It would then appear that to be orderly is a virtue. Have you asked yourself why?

"When you enter the studio of an artist, the first impression you receive is of great disorder: brushes, canvases, jars, bottles, papers, rags, everything is jumbled. 'What a mess!' you say to yourself. However, upon further observation you will see that the artist performs his task with a minimum of movement. If he needs a red vermilion, which has been used up on his palette, he does not jump all over in search of the paint. No. Without taking his eyes from the canvas, he extends his arm, and, from an adjacent table, takes the tube, unscrews the cap, and with a simple glance, places the necessary quantity on his palette. This is order.

"The deformation of culture and values has distorted the reality, or sense, of the concept of order and has rationalized it as being a esthetic. Order has nothing to do with that. It has to do with adjusting the rhythm to the space—internal and external—and the correct placement therein of all the elements needed for working and living. The purpose of order is not beauty, but function. And it refers to space because, in this dimension, you place the things of your world so that you discharge your functions with optimum efficacy to avoid disturbing your spiritual peace. Order means placing things intelligently.

"The disorderly man wastes time. He wastes time looking for what he needs. He also wastes his energy, because he who searches without direction becomes nervous, and the external confusion reaches his inner being. This way, even when he eventually finds what he is seeking, his work does not turn out well because he has lost his equanimity.

"Observe nature. You will not find a tree with fruit on only part of its branches; they are spread harmoniously throughout all the branches. This is order. Likewise, a river does not flow all at one time but, rather, it flows gradually. If this rhythm is altered, then you have either a drought or a flood, that is to say, confusion, catastrophe. In one word: disorder.

"When you enter an orderly room you say, "How pretty!" Why? Because an orderly room causes emotional equilibrium, and it is responsive to the environment. Order is clarity; clarity produces well-being. The devotee who lacks order ends up not knowing where to find God. He loses Him, just as he loses his objective in the numerous endeavors he is simultaneously undertaking without accomplishing any one of them. He loses God as he loses his own intimate feelings in relationships where he does not set limits. He agrees to this and that but accomplishes nothing, wandering from project to project without knowing what is his legitimate place in life. He loses the Lord because, when he comes before divinity, he does not know who he is. When the opportunity to ask a question is available, he becomes aware that he has no goals. At the time of receiving a gift, he does not know where to place what he has been given. He may thus go through life, wasting time and energy, losing himself and losing God.

"Many believe that lack of order, and an untamable or happy spirit, is equal to freedom and lack of ties. This is pure nonsense. You may have fun with a companion like this at the beginning, but you will soon realize that he tires you. The most patient person will soon tire of a disorganized one. He will never pay enough attention to you. He will occupy himself with so many things that he will jump from one subject to the next. He will never complete any endeavor, and he will occupy half his time and yours trying to decide where to place things. Have you noted that a disorderly person also lacks punctuality?

"I am not asking you to become a person who is either obsessed with detail or resistant to innovations. I come back to my example of the artist whose studio looked like a mess yet is orderly for him. This is the point: There needs to be a harmony that is right for you, so that you can perform your duties promptly, accurately, and with an inner clarity. A writer who conceives a beautiful, inspired sentence cannot risk losing it because he cannot find paper and pencil in order to transcribe it before it disappears from his mind. If he could remember this lesson, I assure you that this experience would be sufficient for him to become more orderly in his work.

"If you wish to become more organized, begin with small things. Ask yourself how many of your habitual tasks you could perform with your eyes closed, for example washing yourself, preparing your bed at night, fixing breakfast, and dressing yourself.

"External order conditions inner order. The inner order is an open highway toward oneself. He who easily finds the road toward his innermost being finds God."

Travel Postcards
With my traveling companion Ruth at Heathrow:

The trip from Argentina to Bangalore is long. Three airplanes to go, three airplanes to return. In London's airport, Ruth and I were commenting on how an airplane can be likened to human life. That solid, compact mass is filled with heavy cargo; it is almost unbelievable that it can take off and fly. First it begins to move at a very sluggish pace, then it gains momentum and taxis more agilely on the runway; the final stretch permits it to take off and fly toward its destination. So it is with man in his search for the dimension and experience that may give sense to his existence. Many of us taxi by many runways before finding the ideal one which would allow us to gain sufficient speed to take off. Then Baba appears and takes command; after the last turn we are on the runway. He accelerates the engines to full throttle and catapults us forward and upward, weightless, graceful, and safe. We gain altitude and fly toward Him, toward the inner space as vast as the universe, from where the conventional world, down below, appears small, relative, and distant.

With love the opposite occurs. When love grows, we feel connected and become conscious of the unity of all things. From this new vantage point we can encompass our loved ones, who, by being a part of our most intimate self, may become part of the experience.

The destination is always Baba. The airplane descends and lands, but we are not the same anymore. Even when, once again, we come in contact with the old dimension, the impact of the experience in the heights directs us toward a new way of thinking. Swami says that we descend to resume our learning and growing cycle. Once again, we must put our ego, which still wants to control it all, to the test. But, little by little, we detach and become someone who is flying, someone whose inner self remains aloft more and more and, when it descends, brings along the beauty that has been realized. So, again and again, we ascend and descend; Baba compels us to experience reality, to touch it profoundly, knowing within that the true dimension of reality is the one we perceive aloft.

Sai Ram.

Transcription of the notes taken during our meeting with Doctor Michael Goldstein at the Central Office - Prasanthi Nilayam - February 15, 1991

Dr. Goldstein spoke in Spanish, assisted by George Teague, of El Salvador, who, from time to time, suggested to the speaker a synonym, an idiom, or a word.

The Central Office is a building that resembles a house. The Hispanic devotees held a meeting at dusk in its carpeted living room.

Here is a transcription of the notes I took that day. The reader will have to add to the text the warm tone of Michael Goldstein's voice, the affection and devotion emanating from him when referring to Swami, and the emotional, quivering accent of his words when narrating some of the singular experiences he lived on the path he treads near the avatar.

"We must reflect about what one can achieve being here, at the feet of Baba. Swami does not want devotees to stroll about in the village. He wants us to employ our time in singing bhajans, attending study circles, and staying alone, quiet, and in introspection. In this spiritual journey, seventy-five percent of the work consists of self-inquiry; to accomplish this, solitude is a must. When one undertakes and fulfills this objective, doors open more easily.

"We have made great effort to come to this holy place. Therefore, the experiences that we undergo in the ashram must bring us to understand the enormous importance of having arrived at the feet of Swami.

"For a devotee, the beginning of spiritual life resides in the investigation of the question, 'Who am I?'

"It is necessary that you open your minds and hearts, because marvelous things can occur. Of this I am a witness. We all have come to Prasanthi Nilayam to obtain something. We must dedicate ourselves to this spiritual endeavor, not go to the village and waste time.

"When Swami interacts with us, He assumes many roles, always with love. Baba knows all that we have done, thought, sensed.

Here, with us, is the avatar, God and His manifested creation. That is why we are God, because our conscience is a reflection of the divine. The most important guidance is dictated by our own conscience, because it is in contact with God. The body, the senses, and all that emanates from the ego constitute a superficial entity, a combination of genetic elements and elements of identity. We utilize them in order to fulfill our roles in life. That is how we distinguish ourselves. We should maintain the consciousness that we are all one. If we are able to control the mind and the body and then surrender their strength to the higher consciousness, we will transcend the ego.

"We talk a lot about love, but don't understand or practice spiritual love. Spiritual love has nothing to do with the desires of the body, the ego, or some form of possession or emotion. Spiritual love transcends all that. If we control the mind and the ego, and we identify ourselves with our conscience, we will become united with God's creation. We will love everyone with that spiritual, pure love. That is the purpose of it all.

"If God is love and the Sai organization is love, our job must be synonymous with selflessness, a mission which goes beyond the ego.

"In my experience, Swami is my father, He is my mother, He has taught me the meaning of love. I did not know how to love; I have a wife, I love her, but I did not know how to love selflessly. Swami has taught me.

"I will narrate to you a personal experience. On one occasion, I had to participate in a conference in the Poornachandra Auditorium, in front of many people. This happened a few years ago, and I had to speak and make announcements in front of Swami. I was afraid, so much so that I forgot everything I thought I would talk about. I was crying and sweating. Then I looked at Baba and prayed in silence, 'Swami, save me, I don't know what I should say!' The Lord looked at me as a mother looks at her anguished child. I remember the taste of the perspiration. Swami wiped it off with His hand, which remained wet. I immediately felt a profound peace; not only had He granted me everything, but he instilled confidence and knowledge in me. At that moment I knew that

Swami would always be there, with His hand, that His gift was forever. I cannot explain to you this certainty. It is spiritual knowledge that must be experienced. This experience illumines one, but one cannot explain it. What I have just narrated constituted for me a definitive knowledge, which will last forever.

"We cannot evaluate the spiritual level, nor can we judge the advancement of others on the path. There is no possible equation that will permit us to identify someone else's spirituality, nor his growth, nor his merit. Similarly, neither can we infer anything about a devotee to whom Swami gives a ring or grants an interview. Whether he is spiritual, or whether he is not. It just cannot be done. Continue with your own work, and do not worry about it. Many believe that those who Baba sees are superior persons, or that they are somewhat special. This is not necessarily so. Only Swami knows why he calls someone.

"A few years ago, I underwent a frightful experience. My wife and I had just left the ashram. We were flying on a Pan Am flight from Bombay to Karachi, and the plane was hijacked. Many people died. Three days before leaving the ashram, Swami called me and told me, 'The mind is the key and the heart is the lock. If you turn the key toward the world, there will be only chaos and unlimited desires, but if you turn the key toward God, you will find peace and detachment.' Two days before leaving, Baba called me again. He materialized vibhuti and put it in a piece of paper, with which he made a small packet. Then He told me, 'Keep this always with you.' Swami had never said anything like this before.

"One day before departure, Swami asked me, 'Goldstein, what is your plan?' 'Swami,' I replied, 'I plan to leave tomorrow.' 'No!' Baba exclaimed, and instructed me to leave the next day. As I always strive to obey Swami, I did not leave the next day. But, even though I remained one more day at the ashram, in reality I had not altered my travel plan, because I was able to regain the lost time and was able to catch the same flight. That was lack of discrimination. The same day of my departure, Baba took me in His car to the university, where He was going to give a discourse. As we rode in the car, Swami seemed very happy. I was ecstatic. Suddenly —I shall never forget it—he gave me a deep look and said, 'Goldstein, this is your last chance with Swami.' I cannot express what I felt in that moment, nor can I describe the power that emanated from Baba when pronouncing those words. I began to cry and asked Him, 'Why do you say that?' Swami then said, 'Yes, yes, you will return.' I did not know what significance all this had and discarded it from my mind.

"We arrived in Karachi as planned, in spite of having left the ashram a day later. When we landed to refuel, I was asleep. My wife was chatting with a flight attendant. Suddenly, I heard a noise. I awoke and, glancing over the seat in front of me, saw someone grabbing the flight attendant by the neck and holding a gun against her, while another person was threatening my wife with a machine gun as she repeated 'Om Sai Ram, Om Sai Ram.' I felt like I was in a dream, totally incredulous, not believing what my eyes were seeing. Soon the incredulity gave way to an intense fear. The terrorists forced us to gather in one section of the airplane; all passengers had to do so. We were crowded against each other, some of us on the floor. Seventeen hours passed like this.

"The assailants were aiming their weapons against us all the time. Outside, the pilots were trying to negotiate with the government of Pakistan. In the meantime, while sitting there, I remembered what Swami told me about the key and the lock. I prayed, and repeated the same prayer again and again: 'Swamiji, fill the hearts of our captors with love and protect the innocent and, if I have to die, have me do it with honor, doing my duty faithfully and effectively and with Your name on my lips.

"The fear never subsided. I felt all the physiological manifestations that accompany it, but I was able to be a witness of this fear without being possessed by it. I thought, 'This is detachment.'

"My thoughts were very lucid. When the occasion presented itself, I knew what I had to do. After waiting seventeen hours, we learned that the negotiations had failed; the lights were switched off. I knew within me that the crisis was imminent. I thought, 'This is coming to an end.' Then I said to my wife, 'Do what I tell you!' A flight attendant exclaimed, 'Everyone remain still, there is no gasoline!' After a couple of minutes, without compassion, without provocation, the terrorists began shooting at children, women, and men. They exploded grenades against the floor. I knew that if we remained there, it would be our end, because the airplane would explode at any moment. I told myself, 'If we run away we have three possibilities: to die, to be injured, or to escape unharmed. I yelled, 'We have to go!' My wife ran out, and I jumped behind her. We fled through the door, which was crowded. My wife got through more easily, because she is petite. We carried an injured woman with us. Men forget their humanness when they are afraid. After we ran for a while, we saw a food transportation truck and people hidden behind it. Exhausted, I yelled,'Help! Help! This woman is injured!' A voice responded, 'There is no help; save yourself.'

"I returned to see Swami for His birthday. He called me in immediately. 'Do you remember when I told you that it was your last chance to be with Swami? When Swami told you that, Swami saw you in the airplane. They killed you. Then Swami made a complete change.'

"This is an example of the capacity of the avatar to change our human drama.

"Here is another example: On one occasion I rode from Ooti to Kodaicanal in Swami's car. 'Where are you staying in Kodaicanal?' asked Baba. 'Swami,' I said, 'we shall be at such and such hotel.' 'No,' said Baba, 'not there. When we arrive, I will tell you the place.' Finally, Swami made us stay at the house of a devotee. That night there was a fire at the hotel where we were planning to stay. I told my Lord, 'Swami, Swami, the hotel has burned!' He responded, 'I know.'"

(At this moment, a devotee asked Michael Goldstein if he had been able to experience love for the hijackers during those terrible hours, and if his feelings toward the hijackers have changed since then.)

"Yes; if one is to control his own life, he has to look inside. I was able to prove to myself that my convictions were true. No one knows this beforehand, until you face a specific situation. There are three ways to know this: First, through self-inquiry. Second, when facing a life-threatening situation. Finally, when dying. With regard to the last part of your question: yes, it helped my wife and me very much."

(Now a devotee asks a question about dreams in which Swami appears).

"Swami says that there are two kinds of dreams: first, those of the unconscious, which are the more common ones, incoherent dreams that do not provide messages of any relevance. In the second place are those of the super-conscious. If one dreams of Baba, in the first category, we say that it is a happy occasion, a good dream, but you must not try to interpret. The other type of dream is very different. You find Him with you. One does not have the impression of having dreamed, and there is a message.

"I will tell you a personal experience: On one occasion, Swami told me, during a dream, something of great importance, something really essential. Two years later, while in the ashram, we were with a group of about fifteen to eighteen students, a yogi, and other members of the Sai organization. I was listening to Baba speaking to us about dreams and saying the same thing I have just explained. Suddenly, the Lord turned towards me and told me, 'Goldstein, tell the students of the dream you had two years ago.' During that dream, Swami had given me a precise instruction, which, of course, I heeded, but I had not discussed the dream with Swami or anyone."

Devotee: "How can we distinguish with clarity between the two types of dreams?"

Dr. Goldstein: "If one must reflect and decode, it is not a dream of the super-conscious."

Devotee: "Is it possible that one may know that one had dreamed and then forgot it?"

Dr. Goldstein: "No. A dream of the second type is never forgotten.

"Let me tell you something: As we advance on the spiritual path, we live more and more in an intuitive state or condition.

"I remember an opportunity in which I was very happy at the feet of Swami, as if I were a child. The Lord was so tender that I felt I could ask Him anything I wanted. So I asked, 'Swami, would you let me see the world with Your eyes?' I knew that He had placed in me the sentiment that enabled me to request this. Baba smiled and said, 'If I let you see, you will not want your job, you will not want your home, nor your family, nor your body. But when I come to America, I will grant you what you ask me, but only for one second. If I were to grant you more time with this vision, you would be gone from this world.

"Another time when I was with Baba and thinking of my duties in America, I felt overwhelmed by the work that awaited me. Besides, I had a disagreement with one of my brothers in the organization. I then asked Baba for a meditation; 'I am afraid I will not be able to control my anger and my mind,' I told Swami. Swami exclaimed, 'Meditation?! You have no time for meditation!' Then, immediately, he hit me strongly on the middle of my forehead. I closed my eyes and felt in peace, but nothing strange occurred, only satisfaction. I was feeling very happy. Swami hit me very hard, then he said good-bye to me and I left. I arrived in New York very worried. But I found out that, not only was I able to control my mind, but, during the next five days, sleeping only one hour at night, I was able to maintain an optimum level of performance. After sleeping for a brief time, I would wake up and do all that was needed. I like to sleep, yet I was not distressed. I was in peace. Really happy. It was marvelous. I told this experience to my brother and he said, 'Swami has filled you with energy.' After I finished all the work, I slept twenty-four hours without interruption.

"We must bear in mind that Swami is omnipresent. He is here. He is everywhere. The secret consists in surrendering oneself to Baba's guidance in the certainty that one will find Him within oneself. If Swami clearly indicates what He is doing for you, if He tells you what He is giving you, that is good. But if He does not tell you, then one must utilize self-inquiry in order to find Him and find out."

Devotee: "How do you know when it is Swami who provokes this or that emotion, this or that reaction?"

Dr. Goldstein: "I know because of my faith and my self confidence. To hold a dialogue with Baba is like speaking to one's own conscience. I can ask, before I take any action, 'Is this good or bad? Is this correct or incorrect?' It is necessary to learn to look deeply within oneself. Baba says, 'Everyone is Swami.' He is the highest, grandest, and noblest level that one can find within oneself.

"Swami wishes that everyone be happy, that we use our time here well, that we take advantage, during this time, to receive His blessings."

———————

Ways to Acquire Knowledge

"Baba, in how many ways can we acquire knowledge?"

"There are four ways to acquire knowledge. First, through the senses. This is the basic way, physical contact with the subject of our investigation. You look, compare, weigh, touch, listen, taste, and comprehend. It is an essential stage that possesses infinite variety, therefore requiring great attention. Man does not exhaust its possibilities. Once man has acquired the basic knowledge that permits him to act in this world, he stops inquiring, discovering, or exploring further; he remains there. The human senses are an exquisite creation, but man only uses them in order to survive."

"Lord, doesn't man need to transcend his senses?"

"To transcend the senses does not mean to overlook or ignore them. It means to put them at the service of God, not to dedicate your life to enjoying feelings that your senses provide. Those feelings are deceitful and ephemeral. Transcending the five senses implies a turn of the attention toward the inner realm, to the five inner senses, which are the bridge that enables you to access the second way to acquire knowledge."

"Which one is that, Swami?"

"Discernment, reflecting about yourself. Self-inquiry. It is a superior form of apprenticeship. The knowledge thus acquired goes beyond that which is apparent and allows you to approach truth. It enables you to glance at the essence of an

31

object, beyond what you would have perceived with the objective senses. Discernment is a light that dissolves the darkness of ignorance. By reflecting about yourself, you will get to know your inner being. You will be at the gates of the divine kingdom."

"Swami, can one discern without having conquered the senses?"

"On some subjects, yes, particularly those that refer to the senses. You may reflect on what they give you and on what they really enable you to know. What is the quality of the desires that arise from them, and what use can you make of them on the path to the Lord? Discernment is always useful. So, to make sure that it does not fail you, ask the help of your Master within. He will guide you."

"Swamiji, what is the third way to acquire knowledge?"

"Intuition. Intuition is immediate, global knowledge. In reality, through intuition, you contact the outcome of a process happening in your innermost self of which you are not conscious. You suddenly know. Certainty is complete. Something has been revealed to you, and you cannot understand how you have arrived at this knowledge. But the information is there. You have it."

"Lord, does clairvoyance have something to do with this?"

"No. Absolutely not. Intuition is an inner discovery, the discovery of a truth that, at a given moment, becomes irrefutable to you, just as when, being away from Swami, you say, 'Swami is here.' You feel Him. You perceive Him. You are sure of His presence, but you cannot argue about it, demonstrate it, or even explain why you have made such a statement. You have intuited it, which signifies: to know without tangible evidence. Clairvoyance has to do with siddhis (occult power), and that, on the devotional path, should not interest you."

"And what is the fourth way to learn, Lord?"

"The one granted by God. The Lord grants you that knowledge in an indescribable moment that remains with you forever. That which is essential is revealed to you, and then you ask yourself how you could have lived without this knowledge."

"Then, is one able to know it all, Swami?"

"You need to know only one thing. It is the One who reveals Himself to you. After that, there is no need to learn anything else."

"Is that also an intuitive knowledge, Lord?"

"In the fourth way to learn, there is no intuition involved. What God grants you is enlightenment."

"And, Swami, what place does experience occupy in these ways to learn?"

"Experience is not a way to acquire knowledge. Experience is knowledge itself. In each of the ways I explained to you, experience is the only road. You cannot pretend to know a color by its description, you must see it. Once you have seen it, you may be able to remember it and recreate it in your mind, but you will not be able to describe this color through the use of words to someone who has never seen it before. The same is true with discernment, because the truth told by someone else must be rediscovered by you—that is to say, you must comprehend its essence—in order to accept it. Only the experience of intuition can result in intuitive knowledge. No treatise on the subject can give you the idea of what that is. That is why, referring to divine truth, if you do not realize God through the experience of having personally met Him, nothing

33

will be able to convince you of His presence. Likewise, there is no argument in the world that can dissuade a devotee who has realized God in his innermost self from believing in Him."

Hand in Hand

"You and I are on the path together. On occasion you let go of My hand and venture into unknown territory. You take a shortcut. You find what seems to be a shimmering icy pool. Its shine seduces you, it attracts you, and you go there with all your intensity. But as soon as you take the first steps on it, the frost—for that is what it was—breaks under your weight into a thousand pieces, and you sink into the mud up to your neck. There you dabble for a while, turn around, and, when you are able to come out, discover you have lost your bearings. You realize it, not only because you do not know which direction to take, but also because of the anguish and despair that clouds your judgment and your spirit.

"I say to you, 'Return to Me.' It does not matter how much mud covers you. Return to Me to find the lost path. Find My hand within the undergrowth and hold tight to it. Then allow Me to guide you. I will receive you in My heart, rejoicing with the new knowledge you have acquired, knowledge that returns you to Me with more firmness and devotion. Once back on the path, I will help you to clean off the mud. Hand in hand we will continue to walk. Peace will inundate your heart. It will speak to you of the depth of the love between us, of My continued care in your life, of the responsibility that I claim over all your affairs, and My reassurance that you are Mine forever. You asked me what is our new destination. We are going toward Prasanthi Nilayam. That is the goal. That is the place where you must arrive. The path leads you always to Prasanthi Nilayam, and ... Prasanthi Nilayam is Me."

Enlightenment

"Swamiji, can man receive enlightenment and continue living in the world? I mean to say, interact, work, move here and there?"

"Man must always interact, work, and move here and there. Otherwise, enlightenment would be only for a few people, and that is not so. God is anxious to give His knowledge away. God does not do this more often because man does not frequently and fervently desire enlightenment. Every human being moves toward enlightenment: the knowledge of the All, the meeting and fusion with the One. The majority stay with the first way of obtaining knowledge (using the senses); the senses entrap, subjugate, enslave. Many desire liberation and enlightenment but do not work to achieve these. They are not ready to confront the exigencies of deep self-inquiry and the transformation that is necessary in order to enter the spiritual path. But, yes, the enlightened being continues in the world but does not get involved in worldly matters; rather, he transcends them.

"Understand me well. It is not that the enlightened person is either above or not concerned with matters of the world. It is that he understands them through a superior knowledge that enables him to discern that which is real from that which is illusory, that which is important from that which is not."

"Lord, how can one tell when someone has reached enlightenment?"

"You cannot tell. Not even the enlightened person knows it."

"What, Swami!? Could someone have received enlightenment and not be aware of it?"

"Of course! Do you imagine someone proclaiming, 'I have just received enlightenment'? Only God knows it."

35

The Divine Complement

"If you fix your sight on a red-colored image, after a while a green shadow will appear around it. Likewise, if you look at an orange-colored image, when you close your eyes you will see appearing before your inner eye a blue halo in the same place where the orange image had been. They are complementary colors. This is rhythm, consonant vibration, harmony. The human eye can get used to this type of vision to provide us with a teaching. Choose an image with a defined color. Carefully observe it for a few seconds and then close your eyes. Blink internally and, lo, there it is! The image is in your retina with the complementary color.

"Everything in the universe carries an aspect that complements it. That complement is not the opposite, but rather completes and accompanies it. It is the hidden truth, which, when unveiled, enriches the vision and the experience. It is the other aspect beyond that which is apparent, the fact that permits the deep understanding of an event, a thought, and a behavior. See how much better red vibrates on the palette of a painter if a dab of green is adjacent to it. The orange complements the blue in all its hues.

"What I am revealing to you holds a profound truth. It has to do with simultaneous existence, and with what is hidden beyond the apparent; the potency of action of the complement that is hidden is as strong as the one that is visible—we must not disregard this. There is no love withoutho surrender, there is no surrender without obedience, and no obedience without respect. There is no fear without separation, resentment without inner poverty, or devotion without being enamored. here is no happiness without nostalgia, or familiarity without ease.

"When you contemplate a color, it is the complementary color that is sustained in your retina. There is nothing in creation without support. Only God is neither supported nor complemented; He is the Absolute.

36

"Observe, wake up, and investigate. Inquire into what it is that sustains each object. The complement of the note you hear vibrates in the apparent silence at the same time that the note that is being heard, only your hearing is not prepared to discern such richness. Nature cannot be perfected. It is perfect. If you feed fertilizer to your fruit trees, you will be able to harvest fruit that is larger and sweeter. But you will not be able to alter the creation process. What you harvest is only the fruit which that tree offers—never otherwise. In nature everything is explained. Its laws are obvious to everyone, and their profound significance is being repeated in an identical manner through the centuries.

"Man is blinded by prejudices. He has learned and now teaches that this or that cannot be done. Yet when he sees that which he thought could not be done is done, he still denies it because he lacks an inner structure that will permit him to accept that new fact. He resists, he ridicules, and, in his ignorance, he gathers a volume of data through which he attempts to demonstrate to others what he calls 'reality.' He has not seen green in the red, nor yellow in the violet. He does not know.

"The key to progress consists in allowing access to your inner world. No one can enter when the door is closed, and, if you do not open it, no one will force it open, not even God. If someone whom you consider superior to you, such as your Master, gives you knowledge, do not reject it because it appears improbable. Open yourself to that truth and experience it. The world will reveal itself to you as unparalleled harmony, and you will flow into that harmonious whole created by God's love.

"Ignorance is often nothing more than a choice made when blinded by fear. Devotees are not aware that, on certain occasions, lack of courage (to open to revealed inner realities) is almost a sacrilege. God is your support, your sustenance, your eternal complement. God is that which remains after your self-image has been erased, that which enables you to exist on

37

all levels of consciousness, and that which is discovered with the inner eye. In a word, God is your true being. Become conscious of this immeasurable gift of not only being what is apparent, but also being the not-apparent accompanying vibration which is that of the supreme Being. It is the divinity that comprises the secret note that accompanies and harmonizes with every note in your life."

Samadhi (II)

"Beloved Swami, I keep thinking about being unconscious during samadhi and about the knowledge that ensues. It is still not clear to me."

"When, in order to perform a surgical operation, a person is anesthetized, there is no doubt that the operation can be performed even though the person is not a conscious witness to the event. He only needs to verify the effect of the operation on himself afterward. It is the same with samadhi. You ask me how one can know samadhi in depth. It is because the Masters have achieved this state of bliss and have brought it back to the everyday level of consciousness. From where would they have been able to bring it, if not from the super-consciousness, from the state of ecstasy in which they were submerged? They 'awoke' in a state of blessedness, and they maintained that state. That is why they were able to speak about it.

"Of course, this is not the case of the ordinary mortal, for he returns from samadhi and experiences that the world is not the same for him. He is certain of this even though he cannot express it in words. Remember, the explanation does not diminish the experience; it is only an approximation, which cannot be satisfactory. Just because he cannot find words that totally explain the experience, do not believe that the experience he has lived is as poor as the language with which he is trying to express himself. It is not so. If you wish to know the perfume of jasmine, get close to it and smell it. There is no other way to know it. Anything you may say in order to describe the perfume of jasmine will not be reliable. The same happens with ecstasy: while you are in samadhi, you are not aware of the experience. But when you return here, in the dimension of your sensory perception, even though the experience cannot be described, you know it has happened."

"Then, Swami, this signifies that I was conscious."

"Not from the ego standpoint, not from the standpoint of the ordinary consciousness. In samadhi you fuse with the One; there the ego disappears."

"I still have difficulty in associating fusion with the One and the experience of bliss."

"This is because you evaluate it from the ego's view and its limitations. Even when you say, 'One,' you still think of Him as 'other' than you; when you live in duality, you cannot conceive of absolute unity. For you, 'I am one with the All' is loneliness, because the 'other,' whom you need for company, has disappeared."

"Then Swami, what must I do?"

"Have trust in your Master. Follow His teachings and let Him guide you. He, and only He, must be your reference point. Your Master comes from the place where you are going. He knows."

Divine Alliance

"When you feel you have erred, change direction and become an ally of the divine. This is really easy. It only requires attention and willingness. Attention, in order to receive God's message. Willingness, in order to fulfill God's directives without

39

hesitation. If you become an ally of the divine, loneliness will be impossible, nor will it be possible to continue to make mistakes. The power of the Supreme is absolute, and it is offered to you for your use. If God is your ally, who could compare to Him and who could oppose Him?"

Karma Without Desires

"Baba, how can I achieve karma without desire, and action without expecting a reward?"

"Observe nature. A bird perches on a branch and sings for a few minutes. It does not call its companion, or chase away its enemies, or mark its territory. It simply sings. Its sweet and melodious song caresses your soul, but the bird does not know this. It did not do this expecting applause. It comes, sings, and then leaves, without expecting any reward for its action. It sings even in solitude. In the same way, offer your action to life and do not expect life to reward you for it. One should not suffer for lack of approval, nor should one change direction if somehow approval is received. Man acts and expects a reward as the fruit of his action.

"If I instruct you to perform a task, only I know the reason and the consequence. Should you become attached to the fruit of your action, perhaps you will not be able to discover the reason and understand its consequence. Commence a task, end it, and continue with the next one. I will take care of the results. Maybe at the beginning you will not find it easy to give up your expectations; you will have to instruct your intellect to go without the results, placing your attention on something else and deliberately forgetting about them."

"Why is it so important to act like that, Swami?"

"To achieve detachment. Free yourself from egoistic actions that weigh down and impede your ascent. Act and then turn away. Give of yourself and leave. Do not look behind you. If

40

you stay to observe the result and the result is not what you expected, you may become disillusioned and interrupt an action that was correct. Some say: 'I give, I give, but I never receive. I will not give anymore!' Such determination is egoistic. Such a person does not give, he only seeks an exchange. It does not work. Give, and leave the rest to God."

Fear or Love

"Fear is confusion. Love is peace and certainty. When you are confronted by any contingency, ask yourself how should you respond; should it be from fear, or from love? If you do it from fear, there will be confusion and you will lose your direction. From then on, error is inevitable. If you respond from love, your action will be correct, because it will be God who will guide your steps. Fear moves you away from God. In fact, fear is remoteness from the divine. It is limiting and senseless. Love is God in action. Love is expansiveness. Love is freedom. Responding from fear will make you excessively prudent, sad, and hesitant. When you respond from love, you are certain of God's help. So, be brave and happy. Everything will lead you to triumph, as triumph is the only possible destination."

The Fruits of Action

"Lord, is expecting the fruits of action also applicable to the relationship with God?"

"You must apply it especially to your relationship with God. You cannot adore God expecting reward for that. You cannot offer God your work with an ulterior motive."

"How can I achieve this, Swami?"

"Get used to seeing God's grace in everything. Every happening is an act of His grace. This is especially true of your conduct. Your action is the result of His grace, rather than your

41

motivation to achieve an objective. If you act because of His grace, would you still await the result, the reward? Offer your deeds. Everything else is the response of your ego, and that must be eliminated in your relationship with God."

Travel Postcards

Swami is singing in the Poornachandra Hall. His head is bowed down, as if concentrating on the sound of the voices that respond to the verses chanted by Him. Baba marks the rhythm with His right hand. He does it briskly, with decision and authority. He then raises His head, looking at the crowd who clapping to the rhythm of the bhajan, and then begins the next verse. The sweet and tender voice of Swami skillfully modulates each note accompanied by the organ, the drums, and the tambourine. We try to imitate His sound.

Before I went to see Baba, hearing Him sing had produced an emotion of singular tenderness in me and an admiration for the tone of His voice, as well as for the musicality He imparted to every phrase. Seeing Him gave me a different impression. The dominant factor now was the strength, the decision with which he attacked each note, the commanding attitude emanating from every gesture when He was conducting the singing. His serious face, concentrated, earnest, gave His voice—though still warm and mellow—a new sound of energy and firmness that we could not help but follow.

Untiringly, we spent the entire night at the auditorium singing bhajans—it was the morning during the Mahasivarathri Festival—we were singing with great devotion, encouraged by the presence of this extraordinary Being. Baba seemed to glow there, on the stage. This was the light He made grow in the heart of each one of us that morning in Prasanthi Nilayam.

Transcription of the notes taken during the meeting with Dr. John S. Hislop - Central Office - Prasanthi Nilayam

Dr. John S. Hislop, author of the books *My Baba and I* and *Conversations with Sathya Sai Baba,* was speaking to us. A group of us from Argentina and other Hispanic devotees were meeting at the Central Office building. It was 7 P.M. of February 19, 1991. Thanks to George Teague of El Salvador, who was translating, I was able to take these notes, which I am now transcribing so that others, who were not present during the occasion, will be able to enjoy—as we did—what a devotee so close to the Lord expressed. Dr. Hislop began:

"This afternoon I was seated on the verandah of the Mandir when Swami called me. 'How are the Argentineans?' he asked. 'We are going to speak to them tonight, Baba,' I responded. Then the Lord said, 'The Argentineans are very good people, but they have a dangerous tendency — that of seeking other fountains, other gurus. There is only one guru, and that is God.'

"The small body of Swami can make us come to a wrong conclusion. One can ask himself how is it possible for a small being to be God. The major sign of divinity, which we see clearly, is the love that emanates from Baba toward us. 'Tell the Argentineans to center their attention on God,' said Swami, 'For He is the destination. The destination is God.'

"We may ask what is the main focus of Swami's teachings. It is that each one of us is divine. It is so, but are we conscious of this? Due to our ignorance we are not conscious of this. We have a series of wrong concepts about the world, about ourselves, and about God. Of course, we have the possibility of freeing ourselves from these concepts.

"This reminds me of the Hindu story of the rope in a darkened place; when one is looking in the dark, one may think that the rope is a serpent, or a cobra in the middle of our path. In the dark one may make a mistake. It is probable that confronted with this situation, we will turn around and flee in fear, or that we may do something silly. Where has the serpent come from? From the mind of the observer, from no other place. If one could resist the

43

temptation to flee and, instead, observe attentively for a few moments, one would inevitably penetrate the illusion and see the rope for what it is. Likewise, through self-inquiry, in order to analyze what we believe regarding what we perceive, we could be able to realize who we are and what is illusion. This would tear the veil of ignorance that covers our eyes: This is liberation.

"Liberation means to remove oneself from deception and mistaken perception. Then one realizes oneself as a person, just as Jesus realized Himself. He said: 'I am the messenger of God,' 'I am the Son of God,' and 'My Father and I are One.' He affirmed that He was not different from His Father. He was Almighty God, in no way different from God Himself. This awakening is available to each and every one of us. Swami's teachings are given to us in order to liberate us from erroneous concepts. From time immemorial the essence of the teachings and of all sadhana (spiritual discipline) has been: We must purify the mind and the heart of all that signifies ego, emotions, hatred, and envy. Purify the mind of the idea that I am my ego, separate from God, and from the idea that I am the one who carries out an action. This way, says Swami, we will see that He is the one who initiates all our thoughts and actions. We may stop the ego through sadhana. This is simple; everyone can do it. Some of you may think that it is difficult and have doubts and questions to pose. This meeting will be most profitable if everyone participates.

Devotee: "If Swami conducts all our affairs, how is there free will?"

Dr. Hislop: "Swami says that it appears that we use our free will, but from the viewpoint of God, free will does not exist. For instance, Swami sees each person but chooses one. We asked Him how does He choose? Why does he pass near to one person who is anxious to be interviewed and then choose someone else? Baba told me, 'Hislop, you can only see through your two eyes; when Swami looks, He sees that person as a jiva (as soul, the instrument of God).' You may wonder, if Swami knows everything about us, past, present, and future, where is our free will? But we must act from our viewpoint, as if we have free will. Ask yourself, Where does that energy come from that enables me to think and act? That energy is in everything. It is universal; we are all that universal energy.

"There is another way of contemplating this subject: Let us suppose that a group of soldiers are crossing a valley and come toward us; from our viewpoint we see one soldier arriving at a time. Thus the soldier who is in front corresponds to the present, the one who just passed, to the past, and the one who has not yet arrived, to the future. Therefore, for us, that valley can evince the sequence of past, present, and future. But let us suppose that someone is standing at the top of a mountain and can see the group of soldiers down below; he sees them all at once; to him everything is **now**. This is the difference between the Lord's comprehension and the comprehension and perception that we have as individuals. The way to handle this is to do what we think is correct, using common sense, but realizing that the energy that makes us act is God. We must say, Lord, I give all my actions to You. If we dedicate everything to Him, He will accept the responsibility of our actions and liberate us from their results."

Devotee: "Could it be said that free will is a fantasy of the ego?"

Dr. Hislop: "No, because choosing between remaining at home or coming here was your decision; for you, free will was true in that moment even though behind you was Swami giving you the energy to adopt this decision."

Devotee: "Baba said that we should not use pranayama (regulation of breathing) in our sadhana, and that we should not propagate such practice through the centers."

Dr. Hislop: "Yes, I asked Swami about this. I asked Him many questions regarding the chakras (literally, 'wheels'; psychic centers located in the subtle body) that are related to breathing. Baba answered by stating that they were only an illusion, that there really are no such thing as chakras. I wondered why Baba had said this and whether I should write it in my book, to which Swami responded, 'If I had said yes, you would have started to practice pranayama! Exercising control over one's breath is extremely dangerous and can result in dire consequences. There is no value in trying to use pranayama to excite the chakras. What you are pursuing through the use of breathing techniques will occur naturally if you continue with your sadhana.'"

Devotee: "Why does Swami allow some devotees to take padnamaskar (worshipfully touching the feet of the Lord) and not allow others?"

Dr. Hislop: "Sometimes Baba does it because that is the medicine that a particular person needs. Swami is not concerned with whether we are troubled the next day or not; we are His children. He wants us to grow in order to mature and then return to the Source. The destiny of each individual is to return from whence he came. Creation is the projection of the Lord. His breath comes out and that breath must return. Swami's purpose is to help us in this endeavor. Why should we want to continue tripping and falling? It is more sensible to follow Swami, who is here, and not to waste any more time. Even though free will does not exist, one can choose to look toward the world or look toward God. The truth is we are God and have the right to participate in the play of creation. Anytime someone wants to get out of the play, he can do it. Swami said, 'You can choose to be ignorant or not; when you hear Tat-Twam-Asi (You are That), why don't you become God? Continue with your sadhana.'"

(A paragraph is read where Swami says that the world is full of rice and fruits, but man eats meat and fish.)

"We ask ourselves, 'What should we eat?' This is India; here, through many centuries, because the cow is a sacred animal, the Hindus have not eaten meat. How then could Baba say all of a sudden that it is all right to eat meat in this culture? He affirms that it is not necessary to eat meat to be healthy. He also says that the principle contamination does not enter through the mouth, but through the skin from the things we touch, through the tongue through the things we say, and through the mind from what we think.

"Let us talk about evolution; there are seven salient stages. Initially, the jiva is projected as a mineral, then it jumps to the vegetable kingdom; later a new jump projects it toward the animal kingdom, and from there it becomes human. Someone said that Sai Gita, the elephant, was in reality a princess who chose to be born as an animal in order to be close to Swami. Baba explained that this was not possible. There is no regression in evolution, and, on the

46

contrary, the elephant will be human in its next incarnation. In the next stage of evolution, the human being must become superhuman. About this, Swami said that these are not mythical beings inhabiting the Himalayas. 'No,' He said, 'they are only individuals who are trying to attain liberation. The super humans are the ones who have transcended all types of human problems and act only for the benefit of humanity.'

"From the superhuman level, man evolves toward the realm of becoming spiritual beings. It was asked of Baba: 'Are there human beings in the spiritual realm?' 'No,' responded Swami, 'they are currents of spiritual energy.'

"The seventh level of evolution is the Absolute. It is one with Swami Himself. He says: 'It is like attending the university and passing through the different grades. Anytime, you can stop attending school and follow a different road.'"

Devotee: "What can we do to have the love for God grow in our hearts?"

Dr. Hislop: "You love truth and beauty. God is the zenith of all that. If you love truth and beauty, you are loving God. Baba is God. Swami said to me, 'Hislop, you have a tape recorder, and you take it with you everywhere. But before, when you saw a tape recorder on the street, you did not love it. Only after you bought it you felt affection for it. In the same way, bring God nearer. Instead of thinking of God as being faraway, think of Him as very close to you, as mother, father, child.'

"On one occasion, a Hindu woman came to see Swami. While in the interview room, Baba told her, 'When you pray at home, do not hold my legs so tight, you hurt me.' The truth is that, for her, God was living in her home. When she took time to rest, she would place herself at the feet of Swami in the chair she had prepared for Him, and strongly embrace His legs. You can also have Him this way. God is the vastness and the glory of life, and richness beyond imagination.

"Swami says that, in the olden times, men had to perform very difficult tapas (austerities) in order to come close to God. At that time, they conceived of Him as far away, away from the reach of human beings; they believed that it would take them centuries of adoration to come close to Him. They put God at such a distance, but we must see God as a very close friend."

Devotee: "God is omnipotent and omnipresent. What does Baba expect from us by bringing us here?"

Dr. Hislop: "We are here because Swami has called us. No one can come unless He wills it. The most precious thing that has occurred to us is to have been born as human beings, because only on this planet can we ask ourselves, 'Who am I?' and attain realization through our encounter with divinity. There are different types of beings in nature and in the universe; yet, only man can realize God."

Devotee: "How can we experience a sincere love, without going through the emotional stage?"

Dr. Hislop: "Why are you afraid of the emotional stage of love?"

Devotee: "I am not afraid, it is only that emotions provoke many variations."

Dr. Hislop: "Twenty-three years ago, I would cry every time I would look at Swami. Do not worry about emotions. Just love."

Devotee: "Why does Baba bring us here?"

Dr. Hislop: "You ask why He has brought you to Him? Because of His own reasons. Maybe He wanted to see you; you are a very dear daughter, and He wants to see you. He loves you."

Devotee: "How can we visualize Baba?"

Dr. Hislop: "Swami says that the mind is a crazy monkey, out of control. If we are going to perform sadhana, we must control the mind. Swami has told us for a long time that the best way to keep the mind under control is to repeat the name of the Lord. I began to practice this. It took me three years of hard work, and now I repeat the name without effort. Om Sai Ram, Om Sai Ram. Baba explains that the adequate function of the mind consists of planning and bringing to fruition the plan: these two are the only legitimate reasons for the use of the mind. Yet, we allow it to go crazy, to think about anything. Once one stops using the mind for work, it wanders, it becomes out of control, then nothing can be achieved. If one repeats the name of the Lord until this becomes a habit, the moment one is not engaged in working, the name will come to mind easily.

"Now let me specifically address the question: How to visualize Baba. We visualize Baba in the same way that we repeat the name. We use the image.

"Certain monks, who have Jesus Christ for their Master, repeat the manthra: 'Jesus Christ, have mercy on me.' Eventually they can visualize the image. Any name or form may be evoked. We can repeat Om Sai Ram every time we are not engaged in working. Swami says that the best plan is to create His image just as an artist creates his work. With the mind one can create it all, the entire image. If the image is in the mind, God will penetrate that image. I created the image of Swami for myself through an experience I had. Many years ago, returning to America, the airplane filled with the fragrance of jasmine. I said to myself, 'This is Swami indicating His presence.' When descending from the airplane, I had the feeling of having Swami's head superimposed on mine. I said, 'Swami, welcome to America.' Just like a sculptor, one can create the image one wants. If this cannot be accomplished, then one may use a photograph."

Devotee: "Can you narrate to us some of Swami's leelas?"

Dr. Hislop: "Last year Baba gave me this watch (he shows it); the previous year, He gave me a diamond ring, signifying: 'die-mind.' My wife also has one. Baba then gave me this other ring with the image of Prema Sai.."

Devotee: "Why doesn't Swami go around the world awakening people's consciousness?"

Dr. Hislop: "Baba responded to a similar question stating that, if He went to other places before setting His country in order, the world would think that Swami's task was ridiculous."

Devotee: "Will Swami do this one day?"

Dr. Hislop: "He once said that He would go, but the trip was interrupted. We will know that Swami is actually going only when the airplane carrying Him is halfway there."

Divine Omnipresence

Manifestations of Omnipresence

"Swami, could you tell me something more about how the divine omnipresence becomes evident to man?"

"At the beginning, man experiences the omnipresence of the Supreme without being aware of it. This is due to ignorance. Man does not know that when he thinks of God he evokes Him, just as he does when he remembers someone. Unconsciously he experiences Him there, where the Supreme resides, in his inner self. When you think of God, you instantly tune yourself to Him. He is always there, but now communication and dialogue are established. When you become conscious of this, you have the first manifestation of divine omnipresence.

"When you remember a friend, no matter how much you think of him, even when you pass him on the street, you realize that your remembrance has not changed the bond. Both of you must resume your relationship from the point at which you left it on your last meeting. With God, this does not occur. Each time you invoke Him, each time you think of Him or remember Him, you are in fact in contact with Him. And your bond grows and becomes deeper, because God is in fact present within you. God is present where the remembrance takes place, where the invocation or the idea is. That is why you are urged to direct your thought to the Lord; He is there, He is there all the time.

"When you experience the truth of the presence of the Supreme in you, your spiritual growth becomes continuous, because you are in contact with the fountain of primordial teaching, of the deepest happiness, of the most complete tranquility.

"Devotees usually speak of omnipresence when they become aware of the effect of the tangible presence of the

Lord. We could call this an intuitively perceived manifestation that, for the devotee, translates into a directly perceived experience in some of the dimensions of daily life."

"Swami, what are those dimensions, and what are the corresponding experiences You speak of?"

"The first dimension is the physical. A devotee sees Me there, where his reason tells him I could not be in that moment. Another devotee indicates he is perceiving the scent that identifies Me. A third one finds vibhuti in the frame of a photograph. A fourth one perceives an improvement in the illness that has been bothering him. In these situations, the senses are active and the stories can be shared as tangible experiences.

"It is different from what occurs in the mental dimension. In this case, the phenomenon is noted by only one person. For example, a devotee receives a message. He knows that it is not his, that it has been sent by Me. His certainty is complete, and so he transmits it. This devotee has experienced my omnipresence, but the others, in order to accept that experience, may need the phenomenon corroborated by Me.

"Another manifestation of My omnipresence in the mental plane is produced through the medium of dreams. When I wish to connect in a special manner with a devotee, I appear in his dreams and he receives the message without any distortion—no matter where he may be.

"The third dimension of the human experience in which the Lord expresses His omnipresence is the spiritual dimension. Here, the effect is the expansion of consciousness, the deepening of the intuitive level, the awakening to a transcendent knowledge that now can be called wisdom. It results in a level of communion with the Supreme that borders on illumination. Here the devotee has realized God's presence in each and every thing. He receives permanent signs of the divine omnipresence, and the One draws him toward that indescribable union that is the culmination of the spiritual path.

"The Lord's omnipresence manifests also when He is the witness. He narrates to you what you have experienced, thought, or felt when you believed you were far away from Him. The witness knows what happens everywhere, all the time. He is contemporaneous with all events. In a word, the witness is He who knows. You become aware of this when I tell you.

"I manifest in so many ways in order to give to each one the kind of proof needed for his faith to progress, so that he will not stop until reaching the supreme bliss, which is merging with Me.

"That all this happens at the same time is difficult for man to understand. The human mind orients itself toward analysis, and to understand omnipresence it is necessary to transcend logical thought. You say, 'Swami is omnipresent' and immediately you imagine Him here, there, farther and farther away. In other words, you amplify the limits within which you imagine Baba. You cannot see the all in all simultaneously and always. These are human limitations, which later on are transformed into achievements on the path of the spirit. But for that, you must expand your consciousness. In this, I will help you."

"Baba, is there a difference between the Lord's manifestation and omnipresence?"

"Divine omnipresence manifests always, only you are not conscious of this. For some it is a passive omnipresence, inactive or latent. For others, it is active and directly perceived. There will come a time when it is perceived in spite of your doubts or blindness. It is a matter of intensity and degree. God is tangible to each one in accordance with the measure of his sensitivity, faith, and growth. Divine grace also determines when a devotee merits or necessitates such a gift."

52

"Swami, is God omnipresent because everything emanates from Him?"

"God is omnipresent because He is omnipotent. Being all-powerful He acts at all levels of creation simultaneously. He is everywhere. Being omnipresent, He is never absent. He is also omniscient, because His knowledge has no limits. He is perfection itself; there is no attribute that does not belong to Him. There is no quality that can be denied Him. You cannot assign to Him any magnitude, because these qualities are transcended by Him. Being perfect, God cannot not be. He cannot not know, or in any way lack power. He is the Almighty, and it is through His infinite compassion that He allows the devotee to enjoy His presence."

Vibhuti

During a meeting of the Argentinean group at Prasanthi Nilayam, January of 1990, Alejandro, one of its members, narrated an experience. "We can adopt many ways to communicate with Swami," he tells us. He explains how, a few days before, he had decided to ask Baba for vibhuti (holy ash) while at darshan, but he did not ask aloud, but rather mentally.

"That afternoon," Alejandro (Ale) Cohn tells us, "I was in the first row; Swami was walking very slowly toward us. I concentrated my attention on His face while asking silently for Him to give me vibhuti; I repeated my request with faith, expectation, and insistence. Baba passed me by without looking at me."

Ale told us about the contradictory emotions that were awakened in his mind as Swami was passing him. He felt that the Lord did not want to respond to him, or that He did not receive his request.

"I followed Him with my eyes until his image disappeared behind the rows of devotees," said Ale and concluded, "Disappointed, I lowered my head. Then I discovered one leg of my pants was full of vibhuti."

Always

"The omnipresence of God signifies that He is also protecting you even when you doubt Him, when you withdraw from Him, or when you deny Him. God's omnipresence is His promise, which is fulfilled at the very instant of being formulated in your mind. His omnipresence is never ending because it never had a beginning; it remains as an unalterable presence in your innermost being. It is a living presence that you only need to discover. That is why your Master knows all about you, because He is immanent in you as well as in everything."

The Essence of Divine Omnipresence

"Baba, is it possible for man to know the essence of divine omnipresence?"

"No, it is not possible. Man can only know the manifestations of divine omnipresence as they become perceivable in his awareness. The essence of divine omnipresence exceeds the capacity of human comprehension and human intelligence."

"Why is that, Swami?"

"Listen well: You may believe that you encompass the totality of the concept of 'omnipresence' when you affirm that 'God is simultaneously present everywhere all the time Now I ask you: what does 'everywhere' mean? Does the human being know all the creation, its limits, and what is beyond the limits? Even what you think you know, do you know it in all the possible dimensions, or only at the three-dimensional level of daily perception? Do you clearly conceive the fourth, the fifth, the seventh dimensions where all that is created by God exists and where He is in every instant? If you do not know the limits of the universe and all that is beyond, how could you conceive or imagine God either there or here? You say 'God everywhere...' but you do not know where everywhere is!

"When you say 'at the same time, all the time,' you will immediately see that this is an expression referring strictly to the human experience, because no one can know the time of God. His eternal presence makes His absence inconceivable. If He was at a given point of the creation, He cannot be at that same point later, because there is no 'later' in God's dimension. There is no 'after' for God. Everything is now, forever.

"These aspects of time and space belong only to the mind, and in this respect do not belong to God's reality but have a direct relationship with the essence of His omnipresence. Because the human being does not enter everywhere God is, he cannot know God's time, which is only one, an eternal now. Man cannot fathom the essence of divine omnipresence."

"Not even through revelation, Baba?"

"Not even through revelation. God's essence is eternally unknowable. There is not in existence an intelligence capable of encompassing His glory."

"But, can we not experience His glory, Lord?"

"Yes! The divine glory is the essence of the One diversified into manifestation in matter and form. God manifests Himself as a human being in order for man to be able to reach Him, know Him, love Him, and surrender to Him, thus achieving the bliss that was promised to him."

Protection and Love

"Being omnipresent, the Master permanently watches over you. He sees you with understanding, loving, patient eyes. He is the witness of every thought, word, and act. He guides your steps and protects you. Accept the reality of My presence within

55

you, of this gaze that does not judge, but advises, of this constant company that the avatar offers you as evidence of His love.

"Devotees should never fear. Know that you are with Me. But you are used to looking around, and seeing only with your physical eyes. Then, not finding me in the material manifestation outside you, you infer that I am not there. You are not able to conceive that other dimension where God resides and from where He permanently watches over everyone. Yet, the devotees know how to reach this dimension: through surrender. When you have fully surrendered, you will see your life transformed, your problems resolved, your daily affairs on the right track. In all matters, small or large, God becomes a tangible presence for all who truly love Him. Therefore, love Him and surrender to Him. Then, My presence beside you will become as real to you as your own."

Horacio at the Museum

That day, Horacio was in a bad mood because of the heat. At noon he became angry with Ruth for a trivial matter; this lasted only a moment. Then Matias, Ruth, Horacio, and I walked down the road commenting about our visit to the museum.

Two days later, while recounting the interview that Horacio and Ruth had with Baba, Horacio told us: "... then Swami looked at me and told me, 'You fought with your wife.' I was surprised, for I was not aware that we had an argument. 'But,' I reflected, 'if Baba says it, it must be so. Then, I remembered. 'Ah, yes Swami, I believe that this morning...;' 'No it was not this morning,' interjected Swami. 'Then perhaps last night...' I ventured. 'No,' interrupted Swami, 'it was not last night either. It was yesterday morning when you were coming out of the Museum."

Omnipresence is Not Multiplicity

"Swamiji, the omnipresent Being could be conceived of as an infinite multiplication of Himself. Is it not so?"

"I do not multiply Myself. To say that God multiplies Himself in as many Beings as those who perceive Him is an erroneous concept. I am totally in each being, not as a replica of Myself acting in a different manner in each case. I am, that is all. You cannot even say 'at the same time,' because I am at all times simultaneously, without any possible division, without 'this here' and 'that there.' That would not be 'omnipresence,' that would be a division of the work between the parts. God does not divide or multiply Himself. If I say that 'omnipresence' is being everywhere at the same time, all the time,' it is for the purpose of gaining a small sense—very minimal, of course—of My reality."

"Then, Swami, how can we understand it when two devotees say that the same day, at the same time, they were with Baba performing different tasks, or that they have evidence of His presence in different places? Isn't this as if He were dividing Himself?"

"If you pay attention you will see that each devotee, in each case, describes his experience as having received the totality of the Lord, not a part of Him. The All, gracing the devotee with His divine attention, does so to bring about a particular helpfulness. It is not that the All is not called upon for anything else. The reality is that the Supreme is completely with each one. It is in His essence to so act. God's form, His name, and His substance are in their totality for the sake of each devotee. The availability of God is absolute, just as is His response. Hence one of the mysteries with regard to the Supreme is that each devotee can affirm without error, and in spite of conceiving the infinite variety of beings who inhabit this planet, that 'God is with me, and looks over me constantly and exclusively.'"

Raul and the Medals

After the Thursday meeting at the Florida Center in Buenos Aires, Raul related his experience. One night, Baba appeared in his room in Argentina. "I saw Swami next to my bed. I asked Him to bless me with a materialization; then Swami disappeared and I fell asleep. The next morning, I found this on my night table." Raul showed us a silver ring with a picture of Baba on the top of it. "When it first appeared, it was a medal and it was attached to this chain." He showed us the chain he wore under his shirt, and where there was also another medal of Swami. Raul continued: "I took the loop off the medal and converted it into a ring.

"Later on, a friend of mine went to India. I asked him to ask Baba for something for me. Baba called the Argentinean group for an interview and my friend was then able to satisfy my request. In response, Swami materialized another medal and, when giving it to my friend, He said, 'This is for Raul, but tell your friend that Swami asks him not to make any more rings with his medals.'

"My friend," Raul said, "did not know the story behind all of this and, therefore, did not understand the message. Nevertheless, he transmitted Baba's message to me."

Human Destiny

"Man is limited. God is infinite. God made man limited in order for man to expand toward His glory by having Him as a role model. He will thus discover that deep within every material manifestation, there lies the Absolute as its only reality.

"Swami is in each one of you as wood is within the structure of a chair. Some may say that the legs of the chair are different from the back, that there is a difference. This is only the form; the essence of the wood is the same. Water does not change because it is either on the surface or in the bottom of a glass. It is the same water, even when you say that you drink the first part first, and the second part later. You say that I act with some in a certain way and with others in another way. It is true. The professor teaches in accordance to the level reached by each student, and in relation to the career each student is pursuing. You cannot teach only music to someone who is learning to be an engineer, nor teach equations to a first-

58

grade child. It is not right to say that Swami changes. Swami adapts Himself to each circumstance and brings about the changes necessary for each person. The essence of His grace is the same. He cares for everyone with the same love. With the same zeal He chooses the teachings. With the same dedication, He encourages and guides each devotee. Look inside you and discover Me. The presence of the Lord is the energy that nurtures you. Have no doubts. Be happy knowing that I am in you and that you dwell in My heart all the time. Believe in My word. My name is truth. You all are on your way to My home. It is your destiny to enjoy the shelter and the sweetness of the food I tirelessly prepare and offer to you.

"I dedicate My life to My devotees. No one can ever say that he has been neglected by Baba. It is true that at times I may seem hard and distant, but that is My way to help the devotee who needs this type of bitter medicine in order to heal from the illness that tortures him. I am the physician for all ailments. Whoever I treat will never fall ill again. Whoever surrenders to Me and accepts Me knows this very well. He knows that there is no disease of the heart or of the spirit that cannot be removed by Me. He knows that Swami never tires, or abandons a devotee who has dedicated all his work to Him. Swami takes this work upon Himself, no matter how arduous it may be, executing it impeccably with a love that never ceases. When a devotee trips and falls, I help him to get up and continue onward. He can lean on Me until he recovers his equilibrium, or until he is healed from the injuries he may have suffered when falling. I do not reproach, I help. I do not punish, I teach and make things right. I do not blame, I understand and love you. I never leave you. No one can say: 'Swami has left' or that He is angry with someone and has abandoned him to his destiny. Even before the pebble is left on the road, Baba knows you will trip and fall. Why don't I stop you? Why don't I prevent your fall? So that you will learn from your own experience. I point out each obstacle to you, but you are the one that must avoid it. In any event, I always make certain to limit the damage. Then I carry you, bringing you back toward Me and holding you in My arms, to give you the strength to continue on the path that brings you toward Me.

"Everyone's destiny is to reach the dwelling where eternal life manifests as love. God is love. Love incarnated in order for all to know its essence. Once you realize My essence as your own, you will live in the Supreme vibration that transforms each human act into a divine one. There is no greater Master than the Lord, and He incarnated to teach you. His form is the vehicle that enables you to imitate Him. His work is a message that cannot be ignored.

"To be born is very difficult. This life of yours is an extraordinary gift. Use it to journey toward God. Leave aside the world and its problems and take the road that will lead you to bliss. This is the only reason for existing.

"The Supreme is love. There is no greater glory for a human being than to be inebriated with divine love. There is no greater bliss or destiny."

An Incident at the Uriarte Center

This experience happened in October 1989. I had not yet become a devotee of Baba, but someone had asked me to bring him vibhuti.

I arrived at the Uriarte Center in Buenos Aires at five o'clock in the afternoon. It was closed. I decided to wait anyway. Rama, the cat, meowing softly, passed in between the bars of the iron gate, rubbing his white and ochre hair against my pants. "There is no one here," a short, chubby man told me, "I came a while ago but there was no answer." "I need vibhuti," I explained, "therefore, I am going to stay here until someone opens the door." After ten minutes elapsed, a young woman with a baby in her arms opened the door. "I was in the back cleaning," she said. She told us to come inside.

When I explained to her the reason for my visit, she asked me to return later on. "Everything is closed under lock and key." Meanwhile I kept on thinking: "I need vibhuti." Looking through the door inside the secretary's room, I noticed a large photo of Baba on top of what looked like an altar. "Can I go in?" I asked. The door was open and the three of us entered.

While the young woman was chatting with the devotee who had accompanied us, I went over to the photo and saw written on the bottom, "With love, Sri Sathya Sai Baba." On a nearby table I saw the statue of a deity and a golden vessel. Passing my hand over the surface of the altar, I said in a low voice: "I need vibhuti!" The young woman kept looking at me as if she wanted me to leave, but I started to turn the pages of a calendar with photos of Swami. "Well...what a pity," she said, putting her baby in the arms of the devotee. Suddenly, turning toward the altar, she exclaimed: "Look! There is vibhuti here!" There were two small packets and two photos of Baba! "It looks as if Swami left them here just for you!" She put both items in my hands. "The vibhuti was on the altar, didn't you see it?" "I don't know; I did not see it," I hesitantly responded. Then we all hugged and I departed.

As I walked down the street with a feeling of awe, stupor, and amazement in my heart, I kept repeating: "I did not see it, I did not see it." I knew that when I passed my hands over the top of the altar, there was only the statue and the golden vessel. *Nothing else was there.*

Swami Is

"Because I am your essence, the One who dwells in you, the One who surrounds you, I am where your heart needs Me, where your spirit pronounces the call of love, where your thought remembers or invokes Me. When you become conscious of Me and claim Me, I always respond. My infinite power knows no barriers. There are no possible limitations once I determine to come to a devotee who needs My attention and care. Swami is omnipresent, and He is attentive to all the voices that invoke Him, regardless of the name by which He is called. If an atheist exclaims: 'My God!' I am there. I respond even more when a devotee pronounces the name of the Lord with love and surrenders to Me. No request is too small or too big. God's grace is always available to satisfy the need of the son or daughter who seeks Him. Ask Me from the bottom of your heart, for I am eager to grant your wishes. Claim Me and I will give Myself to you."

Other Subjects

Error and Correction

"Walking down the path you find stones. On occasion, you trip on one of them, and fall and hurt yourself. The stones are there for that reason. You must reflect about the incorrect step you took. In order not to repeat it, recognize the cause and the circumstance that brought you to make this error. If necessary, you may rest for a while; then, with the help of your Master, you resume your walk. But you must not continue to carry the stones along with you. That rock served a special, unique purpose. Leave it there, it is no longer useful to you. Just look ahead, watch your step, and discover other stones obstructing your way, so as not to trip again. That is all. If you carry along the stones you tripped over, at some point it will become impossible for you to move forward.

"Leave the past behind. Discard your old faults and errors, the unpleasant and painful moments of the past. Let go of your doubts, which have already been removed. These obstacles, which have been overcome, must always remain in the past. If you erred one hour ago, reflect about it, learn, and limit the risk of making the same mistake again. Once you have reflected and evaluated the experience, continue forward without reproach. Do not linger on that moment, it is gone, it is over. Seek the love of your Master, for that love cannot diminish or change. Double your efforts, increase your surrender and faith, and make peace and joy grow within you. Only then will that moment make sense. That error will have helped you to become a better person."

Creation (I)

"Swami, what was first, the word or the image?"

"The Om, its vibration propagated in the form of light."

"How can sound spread through space in the form of light, Lord?"

"There was no space. Space was created as the light expanded through the nothing, permeating the ether so that it could serve as a resonance box to the primordial sound."

"What was there in the place of nothing, Swamiji? An emptiness, a hole?"

"Nothing. It was only nothing. No vacuum. No hole. Nothing."

"And where was God, Baba?"

"God was nowhere, because being somewhere would imply that He was in a place, in the nothing. That cannot be. God simply was."

"What was God, Swami? Was He the nothing?"

"No, because the nothing, being nothing, still is. When nothing was, God was the unmanifested and formless, that for which there is no possible description. Man conceives the nothing as the absence of something. But that is not the nothing, because the nothing is also the absence of a vacuum, the absence of a hole, the absence of the absence. The nothing implies even the absence of the nothing. Look: even the absolute vacuum is a manifestation of God. Therefore, the absolute vacuum is something, which is more than the nothing."

"Can man conceive the nothing, Swami?"

"No, he cannot."

"Why not, Baba?"

"Because he names it. And any word always refers to a representation of a concept. If you name the nothing, there is already something there, it is no longer 'the nothing.' Man cannot think without naming what he is thinking about. The elementary essence of man's mind is made up of words and images, each one leaning upon the other. In name and form, you have diversification and multiplicity and individuality. It is that which makes each man different. In other words, this is the opposite of nothing."

"Is that why man is anguished by the idea of returning to the nothing, Swami?"

"Yes, because man characterizes the nothing as the absence of perception of the external. It is through his senses that he makes contact with the world. Man conceives the nothing as the absence of images, sound, and touch. For him, this condition is total loneliness. There, all the senses are absent. The anguish is overwhelming. One of the most fearful sensations is living in a vacuum where man loses himself, because he cannot find a reference point that will return him to his individuality and his position in the world. Only God can save man from this frightening experience."

Leave Everything in His Hands

"Ask me for whatever you need, but do not tell me how you wish to obtain it. That you must leave to Me, for you do not know what is best for you. Your Father knows what your needs are and is going to satisfy them. Let Me be the one who chooses the manner and the opportunity. My vision

64

encompasses all your existence and much more. I know what step you need to take. Ask me, for I am ready to give to you. Then leave it all in My hands.

"Do your duty. It is not correct to abandon your duty because I am taking charge. To leave it in My hands means for Me to act through you, from the love that I instill in your heart. You must become sensitive to the prompting of the Master regarding what step to take. Every moment of your life is tied into the divine plan in a way that you are not able to understand. Surrender means to confront any contingency with the certainty that Swami has chosen that moment in your life for that purpose. Accept what is given to you and stop thinking how this or that is taking you further away from your plans. I am the one who possesses the vision of the all. If you have asked Me, why do you doubt? Do you think that the Lord will give you the opposite of what you wish? Surrender, that is what is needed. Surrender. Swami values it very much when a devotee lays down his will and desires and places them at the feet of the Creator. That conduct is wise. Everyone should imitate it. Therefore, accept what life offers you, work without expecting the fruits of your labor, and, once you have asked, trust that you will receive, because Baba always responds with much, much more than you expected."

Creation (II)

"Swami, did you say before that the manifestation was from the nothing, no vacuum, no hole; nothing? Did you also say that God was not there, that He just was? How can one be without being there?"

"God is not someone. God is all. In the beginning, before the beginning, the Absolute was without space, without any reference except Himself, because there was no in or out, there was only the One, unmanifested."

"Where was it, Swami?"

"In Himself."

"Lord, that is inconceivable."

"You can obtain this knowledge only through illumination. There is no way to acquire it through logical reasoning. Rational thought implies relationship, and in the Absolute there cannot exist any possible relationship. Only a superconscious state can bring you close to a limited comprehension of the transcendent truth. The human being lives surrounded by mystery. Even the apparently simple process of the sprouting of a tree in the back of your house implies an impenetrable wonder. You may be able to spend your life describing what you believe to be the way in which the sprouting of a tree is accomplished, but the truth will always be concealed from you. In spite of this evidence, man keeps repeating to himself: 'I know, I know.'

"God is present, hidden, immanent in everything. He is the One, the unmoved, the permanent, the eternal, beyond any known dimension. Yet He is your best friend and present in you, intimate and ever close, the very nucleus of your being, your essence. In a word, yourself."

Pride Defined

"Pride is an impoverishing emotion, for it hardens the heart. The devotees do not clearly grasp the meaning of pride. They confuse it with being self-satisfied and by overestimation of themselves. That is not pride, that is vanity. Pride is an emotion that impedes your surrender, your caring, and especially your affection for God. Pride is a response of the ego, which builds a wall when you feel hurt, abandoned, or misunderstood by someone you love. Hence you promise never to love again, even when the one who was hurting you comes back with loving kindness.

66

"Pride hardens the heart. Pride makes man cautious, cold, distant, and vengeful. You do not want to love the other who you once loved, because the other person made you suffer. Then you present a facade that is insurmountable. You will not even allow the slightest degree of tenderness to show. You do not give. You hide your affection and defend what you believe to be your vulnerable side, so the other person cannot get through to you. When you feel that it is your Master who has injured you, you imagine ways to detach and become distant. You seek to regain control over yourself. You become indifferent even when the Lord approaches you again. You plan how to rid yourself of Him, how to remove yourself from His proximity, so that He will not injure you again. (Is this not what happens to you when you say, 'Swami does not love me anymore'?) That is pride. Vanity is tinsel and glitter. Pride is a hardness of the heart. It hides a profound sadness, a deep loneliness, a loss of feeling, which leaves you in a barren place where everything is bitter, even laughter. The opposite of pride is forgiveness.

"To remove your pride, you must let Baba act in your stead. Do not try to impose your nature. Let My nature intervene.

"I know that time has to elapse before you can forgive. Give Me the problem and make room for Me, in order for Me to act on your behalf. You must be the instrument through which I exercise My action. You observe. See for yourself how Swami forgives, and learn the sweet joy of the love of Sai, which is always abundant."

Travel Postcards
Prasanthi Nilayam - 2/14/91

Walking toward the meditation tree I hear a voice: "Come, Come!" My friend Rolo points toward the entrance of a small shed, on the side of the main road of the ashram (spiritual community). I look. Two Spanish devotees, Juan Lucas, Sofia, and a Japanese child, are sitting on the sidewalk, rolling balls of dough with their hands. They are placing the dough in big metallic molds. I decide to postpone my meditation and join the group. We are just outside of the bakery, where biscuits are being prepared. Later on, these will be offered for sale through a window by a Hindu man with a beautiful dark face.

We sing bhajans, speak of Baba, and flatten the sweet dough into disks. All the while the smell of freshly baked bread surrounds us with the sweetness of home. It is about eleven in the morning, but we are getting hungry.

We share our experiences of Swami, the first contact, the first trip, the interviews. We discuss the constant presence of the avatar in our lives, and the evidence of His grace through extraordinary happenings. In this case it is more than coincidence: all of us coming together from different far-off places, on this February morning, in this room of the house of the Lord, in order to help prepare the afternoon biscuits.

"It is a form of meditation," said Rolo as he delivered his last tray full of dough disks. "I do not know how to meditate," he adds, "my meditation is service. Bye," he says, and goes to work at the ashram printing shop.

We finish our trays and leave after washing our hands at a large sink inside the bakery.

I decide to stroll around the Ganesha statue. As I approach the site, I see an old lady who is being helped by a young seva dal (a person who renders service) to descend the stone steps that lead to the meditation tree. The seva dal seems to count each step, concentrating totally on his task of accompanying the little old lady down the gentle incline toward the chapel of the elephant god.

The old lady speaks with the young man, smiling as she taps his hand, which is resting on her shoulder.

I say to myself: "This seva dal is meditating." He helps the old lady over to a mat under the great tree facing Ganesha and, folding his hands in salutation, returns to his post up on the hill.

Returning to the shed, I pass in front of the bakery and buy a bag of biscuits just out of the oven. They are delicious.

To Love and to Know

"Swami, what does upanishad mean?"

"To sit near."

"Near whom, Lord?"

"Near the Master. You sit near Him in order to learn wisdom. Wisdom is obtained through love."

"Is love indispensable in order to gain wisdom, Swami?"

"Yes it is, because without love wisdom is impossible."

"Love for whom, Baba?"

"For the Master."

"And if one lacks a Master and does not follow the path of devotion, then whom does one love?"

"You love God."

"Does love for God lead one to knowledge, Swami?"

"Love, God, and knowledge are one and the same thing. He who seeks knowledge is seeking God in His diverse manifestations within creation. To know anything is to know God, a manifested God."

"Does that mean that anyone who investigates any fact in the physical world is investigating God?"

"Yes, that is so. When he finds a truth—relative to the physical or spiritual world, or any other dimension—he proclaims a principle, a law, or a theory. In the truth that he

69

discovered, the principle, the law, and the theory are God. Each one of them is God. They refer to an aspect of the presence of God in the world."

Inner Strength

"Discernment develops inner strength, whereas an indiscriminate mind is weak. It attaches itself to negative thoughts of blame and punishment. It becomes dependent on fixed patterns of behavior, on the need to be conventional, and the need for other people's approval.

"Through union with God you become strong. It makes for independence and certainty, firmness of faith and contentment. Union with God enables your devotion to be solid, strong, and courageous.

"Give thanks for the boons that the Lord grants you, and live your life protected by the sweetest shield, the love of the Supreme, who is one with you.

"When a difficult circumstance makes you hesitate, say to yourselves: 'This is a test, it is a leela (play) of Baba's so that I may realize His presence; His help is always ready, available, and sure.' Then pray, 'Speak to Me Lord,' and ask Him for what you need in order to face and resolve the problem. This is the correct procedure, a procedure that insures success in any project, no matter how difficult. This procedure will make you invincible. The moment will come when you will have no more difficulties; everything will be seen as merely another task to perform. Every task will be performed in the company of the Master with the certainty that nothing awaits you down the road that will cause worry or pain. Some people only partially believe what I say; if they really believed, they would not fear but would excel with that inner strength that they want so much.

"I do not ask you to deny the inner torment that at times afflicts you. It is inherent to the human being to fight the demons of the ego on the spiritual battlefield. What I ask of you is that you go forward with the certainty that you can count on Me to help you fight that battle. I propel you to defend what is most noble in you. I will pick you up if you fall. Swami will wash your wounds, make you rest, and provide whatever you need to resume the battle. There is no possibility of failure. It is only a question of time, stages, and work. I propel, sustain, and guide you. I only ask for your trust, courage, and a joyful spirit to face the battle as a challenge in order to overcome sadness, pain, and doubt. Say My name. See Me in front of you. Shield yourself behind my love, and go forward on the path that I have set for you. That path always leads to the light."

Divine Conduct

"Swami, last night I thought about your movements and actions during darshan. It occurred to me that attributing relevance to myself for various things You did was an error. You did not do what You did because of me. My thinking that You did things in a particular way to teach me a lesson was a sign of pride on my part."

"You are mistaken. You are right if you think that My conduct aims directly at you, and everyone would do well in thinking this way. It is in My nature to organize My conduct in accordance with what each devotee needs and, simultaneously, impart it to each one in a very individual and special way. At the same time, I give each devotee a unique and secret lesson. That is why each devotee narrates something different of the darshan experience. It is not that I give this to some and that to others, but that My conduct is exclusive for each and every person. I can organize it so, because it is inherent in My essence. That is why you would do well in considering each of My darshans as destined particularly for you, as if each darshan is dedicated to you. If you see Swami walking in some direction, ask yourself of what significance is that to me, not to those who Swami is approaching. That is of no concern to you; it is between the devotee and Myself.

"Only be concerned with what I give to you each moment of My darshan. If I manifest vibhuti for a devotee, reflect on the significance for you of the teaching of what I am doing. If I take or do not take your letters, if I take the letters of another devotee, or if I look at you or ignore you, all that has a profound significance that directly concerns you. That is why it is incorrect to assert: 'Swami did not give me anything during this darshan,' or 'Swami did not do anything for me.' Swami has given you all His darshan. Swami did everything for you, only you were not aware of it because you were limited to your everyday perception.

"You are not able to conceive or unveil the nature of the Lord which implies the capacity of being All for each one. Swami cares simultaneously for each devotee with the totality of His Being. That is omnipresence. At each darshan, all of you have the chance to be witnesses of this omnipresence. Yet you miss the opportunity because you are still not totally dedicated to Me. He who completely surrenders receives this teaching in his heart."

Books and the Inner Voice

"Your Master allows all kinds of books to reach your hands. Only some of them are for you. You will be able to recognize them by what their contents call forth in you. From some you will obtain knowledge that is accompanied by anxiety, anguish, and confusion. Only those that your Master selects for you will offer you knowledge and inner peace. This difference will become clear to you in time and will enable you to make the right choice.

"It is not only in the selection of books that I give you this teaching; this opportunity is to discover that inside you is the direction given to you by your Master. You will be able to

72

recognize His guidance when making decisions. A secret harmony unfolds when man takes the correct road, the road that corresponds to the action indicated by divine law. If you learn to inquire from your inner self, you will find that for each step you take, there is an intimate response that, if you know how to uncover it, will tell you with certainty if you have taken the right step, if your choice was the correct one. This requires that you be very truthful, because it may happen that this profound wisdom could point you to a difficult path that you may not want to follow. Man always finds a way to deceive himself, above all if he tries to avoid work. I demand the highest conduct from My devotees, and this will be pointed out to you by the voice of the Lord. Do not disregard what that voice is telling you, for it is always the voice of Swami, the one you perceive deep in your heart."

Freedom and Surrender

"Baba, when the bhakta surrenders completely to his Master by saying, 'Not my will, but Yours,' does he lose his freedom?"

"No, he unites his freedom with the Master's freedom. Therefore, he is doubly free. The bhakta who transfers his will to that of the Lord detaches from mundane desires and connects with the divine will. This is superior to any decision that he could have ever conceived by himself. The freedom of the devotee is enlarged, because it is used on a plane where errors are not possible. Therefore, his progress is faster and more secure than if he had remained free to exercise his own limited will. He who truly surrenders understands this. He knows that he can reach higher because he is holding on to a hand, a force, that propels him upward. Without this help, he could not even plan to reach the top. If your thoughts are of God, God's thoughts become yours. You win in freedom and wisdom when you associate with the Master. That is why to totally put your will into the hands of the Lord is an invaluable

73

gift granted to the bhakta. There is no greater joy than to feel and know that your decisions and will are one with the Lord. This is truly divine intimacy, and divine freedom."

Travel Postcards
Prasanthi Nilayam - 2/16/91

The Spaniards were blessed with an interview during the afternoon darshan. They tell us that Swami asked a devotee, "Are you a Christian?" The devotee answered yes, and Baba materialized a silver ring with a cross in bas relief. He had the ring passed around so everyone could see it, then He took it back, blew on it, and gave it back to the devotee. The ring had changed and now showed an image of Shirdi Baba. Swami took the ring back and blew on it once again and returned the ring to the devotee. Everyone could see that the ring now had the image of Sathya Sai Baba.

During this interview, Swami stated that there were three types of teachers:

"First," He said, "those who complain, complain and complain."

"Second, those who explain, explain, and explain," and "Third, those who inspire."

Sai Ram.

———————

School Director's Talk

These are notes taken on February 23, 1991 during the visit of seven Argentinean ladies to one of Baba's schools in Puttaparthi. This talk was given in English and translated into Spanish by a devotee in the group.

"The most important thing is to try to integrate the educational principles of parents and teachers so that the teachings are uniform. This avoids confusing the children with two sets of educational values. It also eliminates the possible conflict of having the children bring home what the teacher said, which may be in opposition to what the parent said.

"God did not create anything wrong. If when cutting a fruit one utilizes a knife improperly, one should not say that the instrument is bad. What is bad is the way the knife is being used. That comes about due to ignorance. The significance of being human is that we can discover our divinity. Man has forgotten wisdom. When we consider the direction and discipline of students, and recognize their limitations in terms of what they are ready for, everything works out well. When a child is born they do not feed him chapati (Indian bread). We do not say that chapati is bad, but that the child is not yet ready for this food. Children must not be treated like adults, because their minds are not yet developed, and they can easily become frustrated. It is like when one has a seed that potentially possesses everything; it must be planted in a precise location. In the same way, we must consider this when disciplining and setting values for a child.

"When there is a problem with the students, we ask ourselves what is going on inside of us, and we ask Swami for help. Day by day there are indications that tell us whether there is harmony between our thoughts, our words, and our deeds. A teacher must make sacrifices. She must always bear in mind that she is a role model, and she must permanently improve herself, not only for herself, but for the children."

"It is all Swami's grace. Let us not forget that the children are in contact with God, and that His divine influence is on all of us. One must ask: 'Why am I here?' It is because we have a connection with God from many previous incarnations? It is the soul that attracts us here. We all go toward the divine."

The Director wears a silver ring with Swami's image in gold in the center. This was materialized for her by Baba. We can hear the voices of children chanting mantras.

"If we think that life is nothing, life will be nothing. Each soul needs love, but even when we are loved, we are not happy. We forget sometimes that even when we have human love, we are still longing for divine love. It is not the body but the spirit that desires something more. The human being at times has everything and yet is not satisfied. Something is missing: the inner God desires to reach the universal God.

"We cannot miss the opportunity of being here. We must learn from the children and, like them, see everything as new. Our work in education is an opportunity to convert ourselves into better people. The ego must disappear. We, as individuals, *are not teaching* the class. We are all students of life. We must attempt to be better every time we teach. Our tests are more difficult and harder than the children's. We are happy when we realize that we are on the correct path.

"Because of our devotion and the way we perceive our work, we Baba devotees face very hard tests. People may laugh and criticize us. It should not matter to us. We do not harm anyone. We must continue our work. It is important that what we do must never hurt anyone.

"In the past, everything could be obtained through meditation. God now wants us to achieve success through karma, through action, by doing our best.

"In order to teach human values, we need to become one with those values. This is the opportunity that Swami gives us to become better human beings."

Secrets

"Never burden anyone by asking them to keep a secret. If someone confided in you, they did so for two reasons, either because of necessity or because of weakness. If the reason is necessity, it is clear that revealing it will be harmful. Then how could you tell it to someone else?

"If the secret was told to you out of weakness by someone who could not keep his promise to keep the secret, how then could you act in a similar way?

"If a secret is revealed to you, forget it. That is the best way to insure that what is confided in you will remain a secret. If you were to tell someone, 'Keep this secret that I am going to tell you,' why would anyone be compelled to keep the promise you do not keep? If anyone wants to tell you a secret, tell him, 'Begin by keeping the secret to yourself, and do not tell it to me!

"A secret is linked to the dignity and intimate feelings of a person; violating a secret injures those aspects. Do not get mixed up in this; be known as someone who will not accept secrets from anyone. If for special reasons you must listen to a secret, keep it forever, even from your closest friends.

"Once you say something, you can no longer control it. What you said will roll here and there without your being able to control its direction. In this world, you will never regret having kept a secret."

Darshan

"Swami, You have said that we must consider each darshan as particularly dedicated to us. Wouldn't this increase our ego?"

"The ego removes us from God. If your ego dominates, your guru may repeat His teachings a thousand times, but you will not receive them. On the other hand, as your ego weakens, you become more conscious of God's truths, which otherwise would remain hidden and incomprehensible. Prove it to yourself. If you are egotistical, you will notice that Swami's actions either sadden you, make you happy, or anger you, because you cannot realize His omnipresence or receive the gifts that He is offering you. You demand, compare, rebel and suffer. If, on the other hand, your ego weakens, the Lord is with you more and more.

"To realize the omnipresence of God is not the beginning of a change. It is the result of your growth and the expansion of your consciousness. That is why, once you have realized God's omnipresence, there is no danger that your ego will grow. Only altruism permits one to take a glimpse of the divine. The one who feels in his heart that God is walking toward him, and lives each darshan with a private, complete meeting with the Lord has finished with the stage of duality. There is no more ego in him.

"I must tell you something else. To know that each darshan is unique and exclusive for each devotee cannot increase your ego, because it has nothing to do with your merits. It has to do with the nature of the Lord. Whether you realize it or not, He is omnipresent, and the fact that you still do not understand the Supreme does not change in any way the effect of His power. I give My darshan inside each heart. That is why there is no need to come to Prasanthi Nilayam. The devotee who loves Me and lives in accordance with My teachings enjoys the vision of God every day. On the other hand, some who have come to India have not yet realized this truth."

The Atma

"The day you understand the true nature of the atma, you will have banished all doubts from your heart. You will know then that the primal essence, Being, cannot make a mistake. Because the atma does not act, the atma is. The atma is light; it is beatitude and generosity. It is not guided by the idea of good and bad, or right and wrong. These are opposite poles; they are duality, based on actions that seek a reward. This does not conform with the Immanent, whose generosity does not depend on any outside factor but radiates as a natural emanation flowing from divinity. As long as you question whether you are this or that, you are not acting from the real 'I' but from the ego. When you contact a brother from your true center, there cannot be any doubt whether you have acted correctly or not. To act from your true center means there can be no error, and you can do no harm, because the source of your actions will be the eternal, the essence of light.

"Because the atma is the totality, it does not make choices; it is without alternatives. When a devotee acts in a way that is incorrect, he will know that he has exercised poor judgment, not because of the guilt he may feel, but because he has lost the peace that results from correct action."

"In most cases, man acts incorrectly due to lack of

78

reflection, due to haste and lack of control over the emotions. This is weakness of character. It means that discernment is blocked by emotion, and that the emotion is exacerbated because of man's lack of self-knowledge. In his daily life, modern man lacks self-inquiry.

"Approach the Lord so that constant contact with Him can produce the appropriate guidance when the need arises. Become intimate with God, unite with Him, and you will achieve the serenity that is the root of every right response. There will be no doubts, only joyful certainty and abundant knowledge of the true Being. Approach Me and love Me. That is the best way for you to realize the atma."

Greed

"Swami, when can we say we have conquered greed?"

"Greed is not just what man thinks it is, nor does it come about as most people suppose. Man understands greed as a vehement desire for untold riches, enormous sums of money, or magnificent possessions. This is not so. You are greedy when you desire the largest and most delicious plum from the bowl. An instinctive impulse makes you fix your sight on that fruit. You fear others will get it first. You look for deceptions that will allow you to get it. It never occurs to you to share it or offer it to someone else. You just want it for yourself. That is greed. It is not egoism, because your idea is not to take something away from another person; it's just that you want to have it. You think: 'If he can have it, then so can I!' That is the greedy thought. No matter what you see, you want to own it. The need to possess is a sickness of the greedy. If someone has a car, you want a car! If someone has a wife, you want a wife! The craving may be for something material, a social position, a ring given by Swami, a place in a club, an interview with Baba. When someone says: 'I received this thing,' the greedy person wants to respond and say, 'me too!' In this way he is

79

tied to the wheel of false desires, which are endless."

"Baba, why are his desires false?"

"Because they are not related to the real value of the thing desired. The greedy one desires something not because of the value of the object, but because of the insatiable desire to possess. That 'Me too!' can never be satiated. There will always be someone who will possess something that you do not have. It will do no good to tell him, 'Me too!' You will suffer even if you do not care about the thing itself. He who covets always looks outside himself. His satisfaction is related to what others think he has. Thus a greedy person may desire an interview, not because of the value of the experience, but because of the disturbing feeling: 'How come I did not get one?' This is not related to the desire to grow spiritually. He wishes to have the interview in order to know that he had it, and therefore confirm the high esteem he has of himself. Greed is the cousin of envy. Stay away from them as much as you can."

"Lord, what is the remedy for those who are sick with this malady?"

"It is the discipline of detachment and discernment. To want to have something is vain and foolish because no one possesses anything. You can approach it, grab for it, touch it, but the object still is separate from you and, even if you glue it to your skin, you cannot have it. Nothing is yours. Nothing belongs to anybody. The daily use of objects gives you the false idea of possession. You say, 'This is mine, it belongs to me,' but you are mistaken. You say, 'I can dispose of this, therefore it is mine,' and then take pride in all you accumulate. But nothing is yours. Things are only near to you; you keep them in your house. If suddenly you should die, then you possess nothing. You never possessed anything. That was always the truth. But only at the moment of death does it become evident. Therefore, do not become attached. Use things but live dispassionately, free and detached. There are those who are intoxicated with the accumulation of things. But you should get intoxicated with detachment. That is a better way to live."

Misunderstanding

"When you are mistaken, you should quickly realize that you have made an error. How can one become aware of this? If you engage in self-inquiry, you will observe feelings of sadness, doubt, and worry. That is a sign that you have made a mistake. Otherwise you would have experienced love, equanimity, calm, and serenity. When you do not find these, it is because of how you perceive yourself in relation to God. You will be contacting Him out of guilt. That is wrong. You look at yourself and find aspects that you consider opposite to what your Master directs. You feel guilty and allow that feeling to overwhelm you. Then you feel ashamed before God and await punishment. You attribute to the Lord a response that is only in your mind. You remove Him from your heart. You think He is responsible for that withdrawal, and then you are overwhelmed by loneliness. That is when you say that Swami is punishing you. You think that He blames you. You wait for forgiveness that never comes, since pardon cannot come from one who does not accuse you. You accuse yourself and hope that God will forgive you. God does not forgive you because He has never accused you. So now you say that the Lord is merciless. You make an effort to approach Him; perhaps you will get what you want. But in the innermost part of yourself, the seed of guilt has been planted, and that seed will, sooner or later, bear aggressive behavior as its fruit.

"Guilt feelings always generate aggressive behavior that is directed at whatever caused the guilt, whether it is your brother, your friend, your mother, or God. When you attack the Lord, you enter a vicious cycle from which it is very difficult to escape. You hurt only yourself. Review, then, how you look at your Master. He does not blame you. He points to your errors in order for you to correct them, so that you may achieve peace and joy. Only you accuse yourself; do not forget this, only you. To God there are no guilty people, only people who, out of ignorance, have taken the wrong path, and for their sake, for love, it is necessary to show them the right path.

"Approach Me with innocence. You may have done something wrong, but you are blameless. There is no need to expect reproach, punishment, withdrawal, doubt, or pain. There is no need for aggressive behavior. There is only recognition of the error and its correction and surrender. You will discover that I have only unending love, unconditional love for you. It is a love that does not ask to be recognized in order to be given, a love that becomes a healing balm for all your fears and anger.

"You are innocent because you belong to God. I never reject or send my devotees away from Me. I watch over them and guide them, so that they will not get lost. I am with you each day. I dedicate Myself to you because I am your Master, the One who acts, the One who decides.

"To recognize your innocence is to recognize the divine presence in your inner self. Let go of guilt. Do not limit the expression of your true Being, because your essence is Me residing in your heart."

How God Sees Us

"Swami, how do you see me?"

"If you saw yourself as I see you, you would appreciate yourself more. This is true for all devotees."

"Lord, is it not man's destiny to one day become Your devotee?"

"Exactly. If everyone saw the divine spark in themselves, as I see it in them, mankind would be happier. Each one would know that, in his most intimate self, he already has what he is blindly seeking, the One who quenches every desire. God.

"Tormented by doubts, you humiliate yourself before yourself and others, and then remove yourself from God. If you could see yourself as I see you, you would feel peace all the time, because you would see Me in your own self."

Free Will

"You continue asking about free will, that aspect of the divine that you fear so much. On the one hand, you claim that you possess it, and, on the other, you expect that it be given to you, because you want to be free.

"Free will is a characteristic of the unlimited aspect of God that, as happens with everything, has its expression in every dimension. In your dimension you have free will relative to your level. The human being grows and, as he grows, he expands and gets closer to God. The closer he gets, the more he resembles Him and the more he attracts to himself the divine essence, which God is giving him. It is like a generous parent who grants his inheritance to the son who comes of age. Thus, you must achieve free will; you must earn it by the force of the divine presence in your life.

"However, in the matter of free will, you cannot apply the rules of logic that you use you to understand the truths of the world. Man is free only so he can decide, choose, and act in order to perfect his surrender to the Lord. This is where man's free choice comes in. In this there is no delay or limitation.

"Only God possesses free will. You are God but are ignorant of it; therefore, you cannot exercise a prerogative that you do not know you possess. As you surrender your will, choices, and decisions to the divine, the divinity within you will decide, and His free will become a part of your consciousness. Then, the matter will be of no importance to you anymore. Now you are interested in freedom because you are trapped in the web of your ego desires and weaknesses. When you actually walk holding God's hand, you will be so free that, without thinking, you will let your higher self flow through you. Your decisions will be so perfect that you will not even need to choose."

Forgiveness (I)

"Baba, forgive me."

"Have you forgiven yourself? Because my forgiveness cannot be granted until you have forgiven yourself."

"I need your forgiveness first, Swami."

"That is not true. If you come here to ask for my forgiveness it is because, inside you, you believe that you are entitled to it. But if you do not forgive yourself, how could you accept My forgiveness in an inner self filled with guilt? You would not believe in My gift. It would not help you. You would continue feeling guilty and add to the self-criticism, pain, confusion, and uncertainty."

"I feel that I have not yet forgiven myself, Baba."

"Then go away and return when you have done so!"

Forgiveness (II)

"Do not ask for forgiveness. Reflect on your conduct. Discover the causes of your error, clearly identify what would be appropriate conduct in a similar situation. Temper your character with spiritual practice. This will insure the development of the necessary qualities to prevent you from making the same mistakes. Then, search for opportunities to exercise healthy conduct, so that this behavior is engraved in your innermost self. You will see that the forgiveness that you felt you needed from Me was really seeking permission to repeat the same mistake in the future."

Travel Postcards
Prasanthi Nilayam - 2/20/91

Sitting on the stairs that lead to the Western canteen, the Argentineans listen to the members of the group who were called for an interview with Baba during the afternoon darshan.

"Even before closing the door," they told us, "Swami said, 'Well, what is your problem?' He put vibhuti on the forehead of all the men."

"Baba said, 'Repeat the name of God. All the time concentrate on repeating *so ham*. You are divine. You are God. Think of God and reach Him through purity. Purity brings you to unity and unity brings you to divinity.'"

He talked about putting a ceiling on our desires. He said: 1) Do not waste money buying things in the village. 2) Have your meals in the ashram. 3) Do not waste time while you are here. 4) Use your energy wisely. "Sound is God. You waste too much energy talking. You talk too much. Only talk about God."

"When talking about numbers, Swami said, "Which is larger, the number 1 or the number 9? In the material world it would appear that 9 is larger, but it is not so. The number 1 is God, who is the most important. And zero? Zero is the world. When zero comes after the number 1, it has a value. Without the number 1, zero is worth nothing."

"'Envy is outside, love is inside,' said Baba, "The heart is not a love seat for two. In the heart there is only a place for one; there is only a place for God."

Baba told them, "I am not this body; I am power, I am the All."

A devotee asked Swami, "Swami, when I am here I am a good devotee, but when I leave, the world gets in the way." To this, Baba responded, "Surrender everything to God."

Swami also said, "Work is God," and "Knowledge is like water; it takes the form of the vessel that contains it. We must become empty vessels to receive knowledge. It is important to follow the rules of dharma (right action, man's duty), otherwise, knowledge may become dangerous."   Sai Ram

Negative Emotions

"When you experience a negative emotion, use the very same energy in order to do good. If you feel envy because of someone else's achievements, take that as a challenge, and try to achieve the same goal. As you proceed along the road, you may discover new ways to accomplish the goal. Offer to share these with the one you envied. In this way he will advance even further because of your discoveries. Offer the fruit of your actions to God so that He may cleanse and stir your heart and remove all unnatural and destructive emotions.

"In order to avoid burdening yourself with feelings of self-importance, change negative thoughts and actions into good thoughts and actions, and offer that goodness as your gift to God.

"Avoid error and utilize your energy to find truth, but do not be attached to your achievements or measure them in a prideful manner. Detach yourself from all that, and walk weightless through life with your mind dedicated to the Lord."

Notes taken during the talk of Alberto Vasconcelos, author of the book *Mensajes de Dios de Amor y de Esperanza (Messages from God, of Love and Hope)*. He spoke to the Argentinean group in shed 25 at Prasanthi Nilayam on February 24, 1991

The light was poor in shed 25. There were only two candles; therefore, it was not possible for me to take notes of everything that was said. Swami's voice came to us through the voice of His devotee, one who knew well how to convey the Lord's love.

The atmosphere was filled with the vibration of divine love. We sang bhajans and chanted. Palma, Alberto's wife, sang the Hallelujah, knowing that Baba was there within each one of us.

Alberto said: "We are here today because this is the time for a reunion of Sai devotees, brothers and sisters with the same spiritual ideals. Swami says we must now seek to find out who we are. In our previous incarnations we have planned our lives so that in this life we would be alive with the avatar, so that we could follow Him and place ourselves under His protection.

"Only by realizing the divine being dwelling within us can we experience our desire to meet with the Lord.

"Another way to reach God is to help the needy. When we get together as a group, a phenomenon of mutual support is produced. This phenomenon results in a flow of energy that insures that the best that is in us blooms and flourishes. This will result in the betterment of the human race. This is the spirit with which the Sai Organization was created. Swami says that by working in the fields of service, education, and devotion, the centers must serve to bring about the spiritual transformation of its members.

"The individual finds the divine essence through a process of deep introspection where he discovers the root of both his virtues and defects. It is advisable to ask for Baba's protection in order to improve.

"Swami recommends that we do this work even though sometimes we have to combine our energies with brothers or sisters whom we do not always find agreeable. In this way we learn to accept them, to get along, to be patient, and not to point to someone else's defects, even if someone points out our defects.

"The more responsibility we have, the more we grow. Swami says, 'My life is My message.' That is also true for you. 'Your lives are My message; your lives reflect who you are.' We are doing less than what we say we must do, and our thoughts are not consistent with what we say. It is important to strive to have our thoughts, words. and deeds coincide.

"In the Sai Organization, the coordinators, or those who accept to be office bearers, have a bigger responsibility to grow spiritually. They must act as instruments in the transmission of divine energy. That is why gathering together is as important as performing spiritual practices that elevate our consciousness.

"When we are here, in Prasanthi Nilayam, we must ask ourselves, 'Why do we come? What are we seeking?' The avatar gave us the economic means, the time, and the health to make it possible for us to come here. This is a very special grace that has been given to us. Therefore, we must take advantage of every second of our stay in this holy place. Sai Baba has made the necessary arrangements in order for us to stay in the ashram. This is a spiritual retreat. This is a time to withdraw from all mundane activities, yet many continue to do the same things they were doing before they came. That is why I say that we must ask ourselves, are we really taking advantage of each second that the Lord has granted us?

"Swami comes out for darshan every day. He is always with us and always willing to help. *It is up to us to have the will to receive all His love.* If we do not keep the door of the heart open, Swami will not enter.

"We always give so much importance to an interview with Baba. In order for the interview to have its full effect on us, we must prepare beforehand. However, obtaining an interview must not become our ultimate or primary aim.

"What we must focus on is finding and receiving Baba's love. That love will continue to grow in us, even if we do not return again to Prasanthi Nilayam. Hopefully, we will reach the eternal Prasanthi Nilayam. It is best not to think of an interview. Sometimes, some devotees feel that not having an interview makes them a second-class citizen. Such feelings foster undue stress. Swami says that we are attached to maya (the enticing illusion called the world), waiting for a look from the physical eye of the avatar, while in reality, it is His divine eye that keeps a constant vigil on each and every one of us.

"I want to talk about my experience of receiving messages from Swami; it is a special story. However, I am not yet comfortable in dealing with this subject in a natural way."

(Following is a narration of Alberto Vasconcelos telling how, in 1983, after he and his wife Palma saw a film about Swami, he decided to continue going to the meditation meetings. On May 18, he received his first message.)

"During an interview with Swami, I told Him: 'Baba, I would like to be a good messenger for You.' Swami responded, alluding to my conduct as a devotee: 'You are a good messenger," but I did not think that he was referring to the messages. 'Your voice will be My voice,' the avatar told me on another occasion. Even then I did not associate His statement with the messages I had been receiving. Finally, Baba indicated to me with clarity that the messages were His. After receiving more than three hundred messages, I thought that perhaps I was delirious. It has always been difficult for me to accept this, and I still feel it is strange. Yet, *it is a service.*

"The message is how the Lord points out something to us. It can be received in many ways! If we pay attention, we will receive many messages from Swami.

"The ego is not bad, it is an inherent part of our being. We must make sure that the ego does not control us and that we are guided by the divine essence. We must make the ego subservient to God."

Divine Omnipresence

God

"Swami, was God omnipresent before the creation of the universe?"

"Before the creation of the universe, God was omnipresent. He always existed. He is All there is. God is the eternal Absolute. You cannot say this of anything else.

"Omnipresence is an attribute of God. Before creation, God was there, but He was not manifest. All the universe is God, for everything has emanated from Him. Therefore, everything is imbued with God because everything arose from Him. God is the eternal witness. Everything manifested is merely a reflection of Him. He is the cause. The Supreme and His creation are indissolubly linked. God is present in all creation and, at the same time, He recognizes the creation as existing in His own bosom. Because He is omnipotent, He is immanent in all things and is the sole cause of everything that has been created. Creation's of unfathomable diversity originated from a single divine spring.

"Everything that comes from water is itself water. In the same way, the Lord is in each of His manifestations, not in an inert manner but as an active intelligence. That is what is meant by 'God is in each manifestation.' He is present and conscious in all things. His omnipresence is active and permanent, as is His will. In reality, He is closer than anyone can imagine."

His Immanence

During the interview that Baba granted to the group from the Florida Center in Buenos Aires, Swami materialized a silver ring with the portrait of Sai Baba of Shirdi in bas relief. Shirdi Baba was in his traditional pose, with a leg crossed over the other; Swami gave the ring to Horacio Goldberg.

Horacio commented to his wife, Ruth, and to several of us, that the ring had a spot and a ruffled protuberance on it, which made the ring look like it had been soldered lightly and in a hurry. It surprised all of us that Baba would give a ring that appeared defective.

However, the next morning, we all saw that the ring was now perfect. The spot and the protuberance had disappeared, and the ring, as if it had been polished, was smooth and soft to the touch.

The Transcendental Experience

"When a devotee feels that the Lord has shown Himself to him, he should not allow anyone to dissuade him of that certainty. No one can tell what happens to another devotee in the depth of his heart, nor is anyone in the position to judge the quality of his contact with God. This relates to the most personal levels of human intimacy.

"On the other hand, the devotee must not expect others to listen, accept, or understand any unusual event he has experienced, unless there is an environment of love, respect, and a willingness to learn about transcendental experience.

"You must control your eagerness to tell about your encounter with God. Instead, develop equanimity, patience, and silence, so that one day, by your conduct, generosity, detachment, patience, and love, everyone will feel that something very important has happened to you. They will see that something has awakened and enlightened you, and transformed your life.

"Do not speak of God. Be God, knowing that He always acts through you. He is intimately yours, divine, and omnipresent."

Prayers to the Lord

"Swami, if God is omnipresent, can I ask for whatever I need no matter where I am?"

"Of course."

"Why then doesn't He always respond to us, Lord? One may think that He is not listening."

"God always listens. He does not respond when your request does not merit an answer, or when what you want is not good for you, or when it is not the opportune time for you to receive what you want, or when what you ask does not conform with the plan that God has for you."

"Swami, if God has a plan for me, what difference does it make whether I ask or not? If He is not going to respond unless what I ask is in conformity with His plan, and, if His plan will be given to me anyway, why then should I ask?"

"In order to become closer to God, to experience contact with Him, and to show your love for Him. The Lord gives you what you want in addition to what the Lord wants for you. Eliminate your pride. Your question comes from the ego. God is not a program in your computer. His generosity has no limits. His gifts are from eternity and will be given to you simply because you love Him. You have two duties in the world: to help your fellow man and to ask God for what you need. To your fellow man, offer yourself in helpful service. To God, ask Him to give you His very Self."

Palma and Baba's Photos

"I wanted to see the divine Mother, to remember Her expression, the way She looked at me at the last darshan. But I could not find any photograph that resembled Her face in that sublime moment when She blessed me so completely.

"Back home, I unpacked the photo frame that I had bought while in India. My husband Alberto had left for work, and I was alone in our bedroom. Wondering which photo of the Mother I would put in the frame, I pulled the cardboard from the rear of the frame and,

92

suddenly, twelve photographs arranged themselves in a fan-shaped manner on the bed. Each had an indescribable expression of love with which the divine Mother had looked at me at that darshan.

I cannot express in words either the poetic beauty of Palma's words or the emotional impact that finding these photographs caused in me. How Swami responded to the secret request of a loving devotee is an extraordinary manifestation of His divine omnipresence.

Grace

"There is no limit to the avatar's power. The expressions of His will are in effect whenever a devotee utters a sincere request. It does not matter if the request is trivial or important. The Lord's grace pours forth wherever there is love and devotion. His grace will be there whenever the heart is open to the presence of the Lord and anxious to be held forever in God's hands."

Temples

"Swami, if God is omnipresent, why do we need to build temples and go to them to pray?"

"Temples are erected for men not for the Lord."

"What, Baba?! Aren't temples consecrated to the Lord?"

"Men consecrate temples to God, but God does not need them. Man needs a place to go to establish contact with God. Little by little, as he prays and moves along the spiritual path, man realizes that the temple is no longer necessary to find God. He will have discovered Him, not only within himself, but everywhere.

"In the beginning of his spiritual life, man needs many places for prayer. This gives man the opportunity to develop humility and concentration, which helps purify and cleanse his heart. Each temple is an invitation to repent, to search for the truth about oneself, and to remember the true values in life.

"First, man enters the temple to find God, and then takes leave of Him when he departs. Then, man discovers that he can take the Lord with him, that there is no separation, there is no good-bye. Later, man discovers God in fellow beings. Because his vision has become purified, he is now capable of seeing the splendor of God's love in his brother. Finally, man becomes aware that God is present in each form of life. Man can now return to the temple, but no longer needs to search for God. Before, he used to enter alone. Now he knows that God is the One who accompanies him."

Wanting a Sign

I was in the third row. Swami began His darshan on the men's side. While waiting for Him to come to our group, I asked Him for a sign, "no matter how small," of his approval for the plan of spiritual exercises I intended to perform during my stay at the ashram.

I was waiting for Him to come, anticipating the happiness of receiving His look, a smile, or a candy that would fall in my lap or in my hands. These will be a manifestation of His message, a gesture with which He will respond to me.

Baba approaches, takes letters from devotees, and stops for a brief conversation with a lady devotee. He passes in front of me and continues walking without any sign for me.

I feel sad, and disheartened. I continue looking at Him with expectation. Then Swami takes a handful of candy from a tray and throws it in the air, but not one falls within my reach. A devotee sitting in the row in front of me turns around and, with a smile, offers me half of a candy that fell into her hands. I accept it with emotion, but immediately I ask myself: "What is this? Is this Baba's answer, or just generosity on the part of the young lady?"

The darshan ends and the group disperses. I decide to stay there and meditate. Then, in the depth of my heart, I have this dialogue with the Lord:

"Swami, I asked You for a signal that would signify that my sadhana was correct, but You did not give it to me."

"What did you expect from me? Tell me."

"Something, Baba, something, a look, a candy that would fall in my lap. This morning I saw how you smiled at a lady devotee, I wanted this."

"Someone gave you half of her candy. Wasn't that a signal?"

"Yes, of course, but... I wanted something more direct, Lord."

"I gave you what you asked. You told Me, 'anything Baba, anything no matter how small it might be,' and I gave that to you. I give what I am asked. What signal did you really expect?"

"That You would come close to me, look into my eyes, and lift Your hand with a gesture of ananda (bliss), Swami."

A half hour after this inner dialogue, Baba came out onto the verandah of the mandir (temple) and walked until he came very close to our group. Just a few steps from me, He looked into my eyes and lifted His hand with the gesture of ananda. He then turned around and, walking very slowly, returned to the temple.

The Divine Purpose

"God made Himself infinite so that man could experience Him everywhere and, utilizing his intelligence, envision Him in any dimension.

"Good times are forthcoming for humanity. As good work progresses, love expands, and its influence permanently transforms the heart.

"It may seem to you that this is not so, that man's destiny is evil, and he is being driven lower by his blindness and foolishness. But God is active. The Lord keeps continuous vigil over His children, bringing His creations toward Himself. The paths are as varied as the inhabitants of this planet.

"At times it may be very difficult to discern the hand of divine will in the midst of chaos, with nations ravaged by wars tearing mankind apart.

"See for yourself and verify what I make possible. Become aware of the fulfillment of every deadline I have set. Glimpse at the truth of My message, which makes certain that a new project is accomplished each day, not only in the world, but also by the number of souls attracted to My home, to My love, and to My doctrine of surrender and service.

"At times a word from Me is enough to change everything. God's word is omnipotent, and it has already been given. Many of you have heard that man will find the path to his own transcendent destiny. Mankind will unite through love of God, and human beings will elevate their consciousness through service, discernment and devotion.

"Each devotee is a beacon of light in the darkness. Each one, even without knowing, clearly shows the way to those who do not yet know God, to those who ignore within themselves the peace and joy that one day they will discover. That is the destiny of all human beings: to find within themselves the fountain of life.

"There are projects that still need to be accomplished. Perhaps the light is not as visible to those who do not know all this. But for you, My devotees, there is no longer room for doubt. My will is absolute, and My plan will be fulfilled, just as will be all the divine decrees. No one can say that a desire from Swami has not been fulfilled or that His promise was broken. What I declare must be and will be in due course.

"God made Himself omnipresent in order for you to be able to find Him. Find Me in your hearts, for I hold all of you in Mine."

Everything is Contained Within Him

"Swami, is God's omnipresence when He is by Himself the same as His omnipresence when He is with us?"

"In essence yes, in manifestation, no. When God is by Himself, His omnipresence is infinite and incomprehensible. When His omnipresence is experienced by His creation, we speak of the universality of His presence, which is manifested everywhere. God always was, God always is, and God always will be. His presence is the consequence of that fact, the fact that He is eternal.

"When you are talking about the Lord being by Himself, you are talking about the Absolute. You are speaking of His essence, which is the basis of His reflection. You must realize that everything is contained in Him. There is nothing that can escape Him, because He is the container as well as that which is contained. That which is contained is unlimited, as is His manifestation. There are no dimensions in the substance of God; there is neither large nor small; His vision is indescribable.

"God incarnates with the same unlimited attributes. The only difference is that His physical form fools the senses, and you see Him limited by the form. But just as your eyes can simultaneously perceive five colors of the printing on a fabric, Swami can perceive all the hues of the world. That is why I know everything. I know everything because My vision has no boundaries. This is beyond your ability to understand. There are no words to explain or define this."

The Languages of God

The Argentinean group was granted an interview on March 9, 1991. Mariana Kenig, sitting to the left of Baba during the interview, translated our words to the avatar. On occasion, Swami asked her to repeat a word or to clarify a concept.

I look at Him sitting in His armchair, with His elbows resting on the arms of the chair, His hands clasping each other, so dark and graceful. His body is delicate but very strong. I ask myself, why does the avatar need a translator, isn't He omniscient?

This doubt hits me in the chest, but I let it pass and dive into the bliss of contemplating Baba.

When the interview ended, He filled our hands with bags containing vibhuti. When we were ready to leave, an Argentine devotee said in Spanish to another, who had taken her handbag by mistake: "This bag is mine!"

At that moment, Swami came near me and, in a clear voice, as if answering my secret question about the need for a translator, whispered in my ear. He spoke disapprovingly, and in perfect Castilian said, "Mío, mío, mío," which means, "mine, mine, mine!" Then He left.

Other Subjects

A Special Path

"The spiritual way cannot be found on a map. You cannot go to a tourist agency to obtain guidance, nor are the roads numbered to help you to begin your journey. The Master is indispensable, only He knows the shortest route and the special path particular to each devotee. The destination is the same, but no one shares the same itinerary. The Master will tell you, 'go this way,' and then He will teach you how to take each step on the journey. It is not you who chooses the Master, He chooses you, and will teach you what you need to learn.

"You cannot choose the moment in which this will occur. There are those who say: 'I have decided to follow the spiritual path and will begin next month.' This is not possible. No one enters through the door before His Master calls him. Neither book, nor conversation, nor any guru will be of any significance before the right time arrives.

"Evolution cannot be forced. If you wish to properly season lumber in order for the building to last, you cannot force nature to speed up its process. All must be in accordance with its law. A single change in any step would alter its natural progression. In the universe, order is the norm.

"The Lord has a plan that must be fulfilled, and it encompasses all creation. Nothing escapes His divine will. That is why the best you can do is to surrender without reservation to the will of the immutable One who governs all. He who surrenders is greeted with love and receives the gifts of wisdom and peace. These are the only two jewels that devotees should preserve and display."

Divine Attributes

"Swami, if God's attributes were latent and not manifested before He created the world, does that mean that there is a later and a before in God's time?"

"No, because, as I already told you, you cannot speak of 'before' and 'after' when referring to God, who is eternal. The before and after of your question refers to the creation of the world but not to God."

"Lord, I do not understand. You Yourself told me that before the creation of the universe God's attributes were latent. That means that He was not using them, that He was not exercising them, and that He had not established them, in fact."

"He had not established His attributes in relation to the universe, for they were not manifested, but He exercised them with respect to Himself. God was omnipresent in Himself and for Himself as much as He is now. To God, His manifestation is not different from Himself. He is the One, and also the All. In eternity there is no such thing as time, and nothing changes. In eternity God realizes Himself in each instant and cannot die, because He is unborn; He is the uncreated. The act of God is not action, it is being. His manifestation is only the reflection of His infinite reality."

Love

"Love is the only bond worth striving for. When there is love, there is care; when there is care, there is preservation. Thus everything prospers and creation displays its marvels in numerous ways, revealing a single source: God.

"God is the source, and the source is love in its absolute and perennial form. Love is the nurturing lifeblood and energy that activates, creates, and sustains all that exists. Love engenders the sense of unity. Without love there is no possibility of unity. Only love fuses, blends, and converts into a single entity those souls whose vibrations are attuned when they meet one another.

"You will see that, each day, genuine joy comes from love. When there is love, there is no ego. When there is love, you liberate yourself from the ties of ego, and you move into a realm where the atma flows, like a blessed river where all impurities are washed away.

"Man should be diligent and learn to love joyously, with all his strength, daring, and courage. Man should work on himself so that he can learn to love God with everything he has, with the sharpness of his intelligence, with the depth of his devotion, with the illumination of his conscience, with all the power of his mind, and with the richness of his spirit. He must let his body and senses be impelled toward the Supreme who awaits him.

"Love is a conscious choice, a deliberate option, the highest achievement of the conscience. God is your Master. Come close and learn."

Human Origin

"Baba, how could I have forgotten my divine origin?"

"This happened when you incarnated."

"Why, Lord?"

"So that you can grow more. In your last incarnation, you had reached a point where you were no longer advancing. It was necessary to return to the world for you to come closer to God. Your inner self knows this. In the depth of your being lies every answer; that is why each question is suited to your intellect. You came to accomplish a mission: To obtain realization of Me.

"The Source does not forget Himself. The Being knows the waters of the sea you are seeking and where, one day, you will dive deeply so that you will enjoy its grace. The old thoughts that follow you are part of your memory that recalls the home you left. This is where I am leading you, to a home where you will be in the arms of the Father, where the heart finds rest and precious nourishment, and where an indescribable love asks only to be in touch with its inner self so that you may love."

"But Swami, is it necessary to forget where we came from?"

"Yes, to be able to remain here. If you remembered your origin, you would kill yourself in order to return. If you remembered that happiness, that dwelling and dimension, you could not live in the world, not even for a brief period. You come here to do your duty of growing toward the Supreme. Your Master guides you and protects you, and He shows you the truth. Little by little, you begin to understand, advancing and helping yourself evolve, until you die and return to your divine source. At that moment of transcendence, God receives you again in His bosom. If it becomes necessary, you will incarnate again for another period."

"Swami, your words make me sad."

"Because I speak of death. Death for you is the end of the universe as you know it. For you it is mourning, it is separation. But in truth, death is the total and complete encounter with the principle of life."

Devotees in Prasanthi Nilayam

"Devotees come here and visit astrologers, hoping that they will open their third eye so that they can speak internally with Swami or be illumined by some ancient technique. Devotees meet and tell each other: 'Go to the ashram of so-and-so; do not miss this, since you are already here.' This kind of advice is being passed around. It is superficial and frivolous.

"You are here. I ask you again and again, 'Why have you come? Which Master are you looking for? Whose voice do you want to hear? Whose energy do you want to receive? Whose protection and advice do you want?' I will not stop repeating this: My call is not in vain.

"I am not providing you with a vacation or an opportunity for entertainment or sight-seeing, nor am I bringing you here so that you do not miss anything in India. I call you to Me; I invite you to Me; I bring you close to My sacred abode so that, all the time, you will absorb the one single energy flooding you, so that you can vibrate with one-pointed devotion, devotion toward Me. There is no more sublime call, there is no more perfect teaching, there is no better care than what I give you.

"Other Masters may guide you, but it will be toward Me. It will always be toward Me. If by being here you do not take advantage of Me, you will have lost time. Why must you look for someone else to help you speak to Swami, when He is here offering Himself to you? Baba does not need intermediaries, nor do I need to touch you between your eyebrows to enable you to hold a dialogue with Me. Know this!

"You are in the aura of the Lord. His influence over you is permanent. Only His voice must enter your ear, your heart, and your conscience, in order to become the breath of your spirit. If you miss this opportunity, when you leave, you will lament having taken the wrong road. From wherever you are, you will long to be here, close to God, where you are now.

"I am the only Master; I do not allow others. My Light is the only one that can influence you. My form is the only connection that I need you to establish. Dive into Me, merge with Me, bathe in the halo of harmony and contentment. If you visit others, you sow your own unhappiness. You seek in others what I offer to you, and then you become angry if I do not smile at you or do not give you candy.

"Your destiny is to surrender to Me. Your life is in My hands. Wake up; your encounter with Me could happen today."

Inner Calm

"Baba, the mind generates thoughts. But thinking in itself should not cause so much tiredness. Then why does conversation sometimes make us so tired?"

"The fatigue to which you refer has nothing to do with the production of ideas, or words, or even with hearing the human voice, which sometimes can be distressing. Your tiredness has to do with where you direct your attention. When you speak or when you listen to someone, you must direct your attention outward. That always implies an effort. You need additional energy because there is tension when your attention is directed outward.

"When the conversation ceases and you become silent, your attention is directed inward. There equilibrium is born. Looking inward is the natural site of harmony, and the dwelling of every spiritual seeker.

"If you desire inner peace, truth, and contentment, if you seek God, the road is always inward. That is why, if you find that place within you, your outer environment is not so important. You can be surrounded by noise or a crowd without being affected; your inward attention protects you. But if something or someone pulls you from that inner place and brings you into the world of the senses, your fatigue begins. This expression of unhappiness is because you have been pulled away from the center of your true being. That is why speaking about spiritual subjects rarely produces fatigue, for this is done from within. You are attuning yourself in a unique and personal way to your Master, who is teaching you to do so. The more time you dedicate to silence, the more your spirit will benefit. God needs that calm space to make Himself understood."

Mirror and Reflection

"Human beings always expect something from whomever they meet. The first thing they desire and expect is acceptance. To be accepted by the other person means that no one will judge you before getting to know you, that no one will reject you at first sight, saying, 'I don't like him (or her),' and then close the door of his heart to you.

"When you meet someone for the first time, it is very important for you to become conscious of what you have to offer. What do they receive from you? Fear? Distrust? Indifference? Or do they, on the other hand, find an available channel that connects them directly with your divine essence, that does not judge, that accepts and facilitates contact with another person?

"There is a truth that you must incorporate as an axiom: 'Only after you have known someone long enough can you legitimately choose to stay away from him because of aspects of his personality that do not resonate with your spiritual path.'

"You reject or say that you do not like a person when that person represents a danger to you. Maybe you feel his presence will overshadow you, making you compete for the love and admiration of someone in your group. Perhaps, by his conduct, the person you are rejecting is only showing you aspects of yourself that you do not like, and which you would prefer to forget. Perhaps his conduct is the opposite of yours, and you feel that you should be conducting yourself impeccably, as he does. Because of your fear or ignorance you have not yet been able to do this. That is the reason this person always represents a danger to you.

"Now I ask you, what is your basic reaction when meeting a new person? Reflect deeply about this, for the other person is the mirror of your own self. He is placed in front of you so that you will see the size of your ego as well as the conflicts within yourself that are still unresolved.

"Only after you have known yourself deeply will you have the right to withdraw from somebody because of some negative characteristic he may possess. But first you must be sure that the trait that you reject is not present in your own conduct. Of course, once you know yourself, you will no longer reject anyone. You will have found the essence that will tell you that your soul is one with the soul of your brother. You will see that the other person's errors are opportunities to help you. They are being offered to you with God's infinite love. He is nourishing you constantly so that, in turn, you can offer your love without reservation, calculation, or measurement.

"Each new encounter is both a challenge and an opportunity. It is a challenge to your ego, to your controlling impulses, your fear of surrendering, your fear of allowing another person into that intimate space that you claim is yours. Every encounter is an opportunity to get to know yourself through the eyes of the other person. Being a reflection of your own inner self, he brings you the opportunity to discover your own truth.

"I tell all of you that each new person who approaches you is another form of God. He is a unique manifestation of God's spark who wants to be recognized.

"I tell My devotees that it is Swami Himself whom you receive when you meet someone for the first time."

Dharma

"Swami, in our daily affairs, how can we know what is the dharma in all situations, even for the smallest act?"

"First of all, there is neither big nor small. You cannot judge either the magnitude of a dharmic action or its importance in your life or in the life of someone else. Nor can you evaluate the place it has in God's plan. Therefore, no matter how trivial it may seem to you, you must consider each act as essential. Could you say that in a pearl necklace there are some pearls that are less important? Remove any of them and you change the entire effect. It is the same with your actions."

"Baba, I have felt that certain decisions were more vital than others, that some could change the direction of my life."

"It is true; but this is not applicable to dharma. What directs you toward the correct action cannot be decided by choosing what is important or what is not. To do so would only be self-serving. You would act correctly in what you thought was profitable, and you would not put much effort into matters that you considered secondary. Dharma is absolute. It is a mandate, an indelible seal that must be an integral part of each human act. There can be no exceptions. Now, you were asking Me how to identify whether you are acting correctly or not in each action. Isn't that so?"

"Yes, Swami, that is what I want to know."

"Good. In every learning situation, identifying dharma is a process. It entails a process of acquiring knowledge, sensitivity, discrimination, and being in harmony. First of all, you must know what is dharmic and refer it to your life, to your activities and interests, both now and in the future. You must relate it to your relationship to yourself, to others, and also to Me. Read about dharma and practice it. Nourish your spirit and enrich your conscience with the fundamental and eternal truths. These truths are proclaimed by all the scriptures, the books of the sages, and in the word and example of your Master.

"Secondly, you must become sensitive, so that your entire being is alert to the signs needed to constantly guide you as to whether a decision you have made is correct or incorrect. You

106

must learn to distinguish sensations, sentiments, thoughts, and emotions that accompany each experience until you are able to obtain the precise information needed to direct you. This is self-knowledge, self-inquiry, an unrelenting clarification of the truth existing in the depth of your own inner self.

"The third point about dharma is discrimination. This requires that you stay alert, examining with discrimination everything you do in every moment of your life. Are you acting from ego, or from the spirit of the Lord dwelling within you? If you act from the ego, it is likely that dharma will not be fulfilled, because the ego world is the pursuit of passion and self-interest and the search for the ephemeral. It is a world of possessiveness and violence, seeking only to please itself, and the trivial enjoyment of the senses. (You can achieve a sense of transcendence through the senses, but this kind of transcendence is not important). The ego is superficiality, pride, fear, and anger. It is the lack of love. If, on the other hand, you choose to act from God, the immediate result is the attainment of peace. There is no contradiction. In your innermost self, there will be harmony, and there will be health. Then there are no doubts."

"And, Lord, what if I still doubt before making a decision?"

"Give Me your doubt, and let Me act through you. This requires that you let go of your worry and the need to search, and that you develop the fourth aspect of attunement."

"What must I attune to, Swami?"

"Attune to Me. When you give yourself to Me, and let me act through you, you will be able to clearly identify when I am taking you by the hand. There are some devotees who have this sense so developed that they even feel my hand on their backs propelling them to walk in a specific direction. They do not doubt, they walk with confidence. They know that the hand they feel is My hand, and they do not let the mind intervene with questions or distrust. When you attune to the Lord, something happens to you. There is a subtle change in the perception of your surroundings, or there is the feeling of a lump in your throat, or an inner certainty of My presence and company, which is always with you. In that instant, My presence becomes active and pertinent to the fulfillment of a particular objective where you need help. The development of attunement enables you to live with awareness of My omnipresence. This is my gift to each devotee: to experience My presence in him, with him, and for him in each moment of his life."

Travel Postcards

On the verandah of the mandir in Prasanthi Nilayam, the students wait for Swami, as we all do. We wait for His benediction and His darshan. A young boy of about twelve covers one of his eyes, showing signs that he is suffering.

Baba appears through the door of the interview room, walks toward the group of students, and asks the boy to approach Him. The boy comes up to the front and kneels before Swami. The Lord instructs him to hold His left hand while, with His right, Baba slowly caresses the student's eye, repeatedly passing his thumb over his eyelid.

It is impossible not to experience the love that Swami showers on the young boy as He heals his ailing eye. The student appears to us as the very image of devotion and surrender, with his face lifted toward Baba, eyes closed, with his hands holding the left hand of the Lord.

I do not remember having ever perceived a silence as deep as in that moment.

I believe that after that day, everybody's eyes were able to see better.

Harmony with the Divine

"To be in harmony with God requires practice. If you remember the Lord once a week, it is unlikely that you will feel His immanent presence each day, or realize His constant care, or be able to decipher His message. If you only dedicate a period of time each day to be with God, then the rest of the time you will not be able to perceive Him. However, if you continuously open your heart to the endless flow of His grace, if you become absorbed in His sound that repeats within you, if at every instant you allow yourself to be illumined by His fountain of energy that flows from your very heart, if you perform each act, conscious that it is His will and not yours, if you permanently open yourself to the warmth of His love, the unquestionable evidence of His presence in you will be constant.

"The time for the Lord is not an hour a week. The time for the Lord is all the time. This is the surrender I expect from you."

The Ego

"Baba, how can I know if I am acting from the ego?"

"The devotees fall easily into the trap of the ego. They think they are humble or modest, and they feel satisfaction. That satisfaction comes from the ego. They reward themselves by feeling good about themselves. These rewards are granted by the ego. That is the trap, but you do not know that you are in it, and that is why it is so dangerous."

"What should I do then, Baba? If I want to analyze myself, I must be conscious of what I did well or what I did poorly."

"Correct. You must be absolutely crystal clear in appraising your actions. When you did something poorly, then realize that you did it. When you did something well, then know that God did it. If everyday, due to God's grace, you become more open

109

and let the Lord act through you, then you will no longer need to evaluate whether you acted well or not. The flute, conscious of the divine breath, does not attribute to itself the beauty of the music."

"But, Lord, isn't saying 'God did it, not I,' a way of being satisfied with one's spiritual advancement? It appears that way when I tell that to someone else."

"Why would you talk about this? Who would you tell it to? To someone so that he may praise you? If you tell it for that reason, you act from the ego. You should not say or show anything to anyone! Your work is with your Master, with no one else. Do you understand this? If someone praises your work, just tell him 'thank you' and direct both your attention to something else. If you say 'I do not deserve this, God does everything', you are giving the other person a chance to admire your detachment and modesty. This is ego. It is as if you are afraid that the other person may think you are conceited, and so you show them the opposite. Wake up! Thank the Lord for acting through you, and then keep quiet."

Spiritual Growth

"You say you have no evidence about several things. It is logical. You do not know where to look. You believe that the result of your spiritual work will be given to you, ushered in amidst trumpets and cymbals playing celestial music. No. Heaven is always internal, and the hymns reverberate in the depth of the conscience expanding toward the spirit.

"The change will be subtle and permanent. You must pay attention and be calm, contemplating the change in your viewpoint, which will be the first indication of your growth. No one will notice this. Do not expect applause for your advancement and conduct. The work is between you and your Master, and the fruits are His. He is the one who knows what is best for you.

"Little by little love will rain on you as you allow the space for it. If inside you are preoccupied with anger, hate, and distrust, there will be no room for love. I will cleanse you with My energy and with the tasks I give you. That is your spiritual work: to allow more and more space to love until there is nothing in you but love."

God, the Absolute Being

"Swami, does the Absolute Being include non-being? If non-being is a state of being, it must then be included in the Absolute Being, who encompasses everything."

"The Absolute Being is totally inclusive, including both the unmanifested and the manifested. All acts of creation begin from the manifested arising out of the unmanifested. In God's time, this is not sequential but simultaneous.

"What you see is incomplete, even though it appears to have everything; no state that you perceive can coexist with its opposite. Each state of being is only half the Absolute's potential. The Absolute is totality itself, where everything happens at the same time. Nothing in nature can be and not be at the same time. That is why it is impossible for man to have total knowledge. On the other hand, God includes within Himself both the manifested and the unmanifested, the being and the non-being. Even when there is no evidence of the Supreme, It is not absent. If God did not include the form and the formless, He would not be complete. But in the unmanifested God there is still the Supreme as absolute essence. This is another one of the Lord's mysteries."

Prayer

"Sensitive to someone's problem or needs, you pray on his behalf. You take the initiative and ask God to grant him grace. That is not the correct way to proceed. Pray for yourself, and, when you have gotten what you asked for, share it. Do not pray on someone else's behalf. Do not do his job. Teach him the ritual you consider appropriate; show him how to organize his prayer, and guide him so he will know how to pray. Then let him decide whether to pray or not. Let him decide whether or not he wants to be responsible for receiving God's gifts. If you pray for someone who is not ready to receive, your energy will have been used badly, and you will not have done him a favor.

"Besides, this can also make your faith unstable, because God will not give until the right time. If you become aware that the Lord has not granted what you have asked, you may interpret it as His lack of response to you. You may think He did not listen to you or pay attention to your prayer, instead of understanding that the need must be felt by the one you are praying for, not by you.

"I understand your intention, it is generous, but you must change your prayer. Simply say: 'Baba, I put this brother or sister in your hands,' and leave them to Me knowing that their destiny is My task, and that Swami always grants to each one whatever he needs to come to God."

Inner Strength

"Swami, how does one obtain inner strength?"

"Focus your attention away from yourself, toward others and toward service. Excessive self-consciousness weakens you. He who is always self-conscious becomes cautious and self-absorbed, as if he were a fragile jewel that can be harmed by anything. Forget yourself and do your duty. Just maintain a calm watch that you do not harm anyone, that is all.

"Self-inquiry, looking deeply into yourself, is useful while performing your sadhana (spiritual discipline). Do not become self-involved or feel sorry for yourself. Look uncompromisingly at your faults, and be relentless with your inner work. Ask God for His strength. Nourish yourself with the divine sustenance

112

and be happy."

Contact with the World

"Many devotees find it difficult to remain unaffected by the world. When they finish their daily sadhana or return to their homes from a spiritual retreat, or from Prasanthi Nilayam, they reenter the world and become involved in it. In this way, they lose continuity in their contact with me, that is to say, they lose their peace. Becoming involved with worldly matters means being tied to sensual pleasures, to enjoying luxury and comforts, and desiring to acquire money. Some people say, 'Who, me? I'm not involved in worldly matters.'

"When I say that the devotee becomes involved in the world, I refer to allowing yourself to be caught up in daily pressures, losing that alert state of mind essential for being able to react in the moment. Usually, the devotee does not see this as conflicting with his spiritual path, nor does he think it is as harmful as being dependent on mundane matters.

"I refer to daily pressures as follows: focusing on the news, which constantly goes around in circles, to the fast rhythm of today's life, to the inertia of a compulsory daily routine where the whole day is spent without a small period of meditation and a genuine encounter with God. It is daily pressure when people become accustomed to being directly or indirectly harassed, when people perform senseless jobs, or when there is lack of generosity, service, happiness, or love.

"How much of the news that you heard or read last week, that touched or concerned you, is relevant today? How much has it changed your life? Have you derived contentment? Why do you read those journals plagued with lies? Do you really believe that you are getting knowledge? Look at them to see how many miracles are reported, how many lives have been saved by human effort, how many children have been born that day, how much teaching is offered in the homes, schools, and temples. Why do you think you are more informed when

113

you know the faults of a politician, or the number of victims resulting from human violence, or how many books have been edited today?

"Man is deeply confused. He feels the pressure and caves in. His friends push him, his relatives push him, his coworkers push him, and he follows like a poor little lamb, sitting in front of the television in order to learn what has happened in the outside world. He hurries like everyone, gets tired like everyone, and one day he dies like everyone, never getting to know why he lived.

"My devotees have a mission that cannot be delayed: realize that the food for the mind must be strictly controlled, that daily rhythms must be associated with nature, that work, whatever it may be, is an offering to God. Each being is a manifestation of the divine. Only through love and service can devotees come near to Me. In that nearness they will achieve an unalterable peace which will radiate from them toward humanity.

"I know that it is not easy to voluntarily withdraw from mundane pressures when one must remain in the world. But that is my task: to train you so that, in turn, you may transform your environment. Know that you can count on My immediate and complete help. Give your will to Me. I will act for you, generating the changes I deem necessary in order to attain the desired goal. No one will be able to oppose it. Act from Me without losing, even for an instant, the notion of this alliance. This is meditation of the highest level, permanent sadhana, which will make you invincible on the Lord's path.

"But I also tell you: do not be afraid of the world. All is My manifestation. Everything is subject to discrimination and knowledge. Obstacles on the road promote spiritual growth and lead you toward Me.

"Know the world, know it profoundly. Then transcend that maya and, even when being in it, act from the certainty of the grace and communication with Me. I sustain you. I sustain, motivate, protect, and accompany each and every one of you.

114

"Do not be afraid of the world. Change it. Each one of My devotees must be like the light of a beacon on the side of a mountain on a moonless night. All the eyes will look at it, and the shadows will be powerless, impotent. Remember that there are no small lights, all of them dominate the darkness. That light in you is Me. Become conscious of this forever."

Freedom

"Swami, what must I do to attain inner freedom?"

"Freedom is attained through the realization of unity. If you see God in everything, you do not need any temple, ceremony, or rite. If you are one with Him, you become all the infinite possibilities. You become the doorway to all His manifestations. You become love. Then you do not seek God, but experience Him continuously. And all that you see, even with the limited human perception, becomes understandable. Even the most absurd or disreputable has a place in your enlightened buddhi (higher mind). Thus, you reject nothing, nor do you ask for anything. You joyously attune yourself to the cycle of life, knowing that this is a necessary stage for your evolution. But you do not bind yourself. You are bound to the highest. Nothing else attracts you or interests you, but you do not abandon anything. You play the role that God gives you, and enjoy it. You do not hold on to the Lord's daily gifts; you thank Him, and share them with those around you.

"The devotee who is truly free can come and go. His home is everywhere. He takes all that the world has to offer, knowing that each thing is another form of God, which he has within himself. There is no mud that can contaminate him, because that mud is God and he is thankful for it. That is why the devotee who is free is not demanding, but detached. He does not ask anything from God. He already possesses Him! His entire life is a form of adoration to the Being he loves. He then offers to that Being, who is within him, his best, in the form of service. He comes and goes and moves about. But, he is never alone, he is always with God."

"Swami, does such a person need to see Your physical form?"

"Of course, and he benefits the most by that vision."

"Why, Lord?"

"Because he incorporates it into his life in the fullest and truest sense. He lets himself be transformed by the divine without allowing the human form to confuse him. The devotee who is free within is completely with Me in an intimate way. When he receives My darshan, he nourishes the tree of love, the tree that renders its fruit in the spirit and service to others. The equation is quite simple: the more the surrender, the more the freedom; the more the freedom, the more the surrender. The result of this is unity."

How Does God Help?

"You asked for help. You wanted to change some aspects that you identified as impeding your spiritual growth. Your evaluation was correct, and so I helped you. I put you to the test, and you failed them all.

"You wanted to control your tendency toward anger. In order to help you I generated a profound anger within you and put you in situations that would support your anger. But there you went, freely venting your anger impulsively against everyone, with total lack of control.

"You asked my help to be able to control your tongue. I responded by increasing your appetite, as well as your hunger, for words. You spoke indiscriminately, and you consumed everything in sight!

"You then turned to Me and exclaimed, 'Swami, why is this!? I asked for Your help in order to grow and find myself. Now I find all my negative inclinations and tendencies more

116

alive than ever, when I thought I had almost overcome them!'

"I will explain what happened. You asked for My help and I gave it to you. I put you in a situation to confront those things you wanted to erase from your existence: anger, rashness, speaking too much, gluttony. I put a deliberate emphasis on those points where you would have the opportunity to work on overcoming them. All the obstacles that Swami placed in your way were there for you to learn to avoid them.

"But you got caught on all of them. Do you know why? Because, in reality, you did not expect My help. You expected Me to free you, without further ado, from those aspects that you have not yet resolved.

"Of course, I can do this just by deciding it. I can eliminate any negative tendency suffered by a devotee. My grace can do it all. But you did not ask Me that. You asked Me for help. I give My help by offering the devotee opportunities to learn by developing new ways of responding. In this way, he grows through his experience.

"How would you overcome your anger if I did not confront you with that which fosters it? How would you resolve your gluttony if I did not exacerbate your appetite for those delicacies which you like most?

"Those are occasions to learn and to be alert, to apply the calm concern that can show you where the stimulus is that triggers your response. This will show you how to put into effect detachment, discrimination, and a conduct that opposes your habitual tendencies.

"If the Master does not pose problems, the student does not learn. I help by providing the occasion to learn. Keep that in mind.

"Swami will always respond. The Lord always helps. I do it by giving you the opportunity to work seriously on yourself, by practicing, making mistakes, and trying again, so that you can solidify your transformation by your effort. Without effort, spiritual achievement is impossible.

"Accept the challenge, do not escape the difficulty, face it with detachment and courage. Never give up. Growing is a process that never ends, and, before each triumph, you must think what other tests will come along with it.

"The love of the Lord puts obstacles in your way. I want you to progress so that you may know you have an alliance with Me. So, be fearless, no matter how difficult the obstacles you find in your way. The way is God and leads you to God. And Swami will be with you."

Travel Postcards
Prasanthi Nilayam 3/3/91

Group No. 4 from Argentina chants the Om sitting in a circle under the new moon, behind the round buildings, (circular buildings with rooms for devotees).

From the other side of the ashram, in the sky over the hills, there are fiery lines that look like rivers of lava.

In the canteen, devotees eat potato salad, carrots, string beans, spaghetti with yellow gravy, and a sweet for dessert.

The bookstore, offices, and the Post Office in the ashram are open.

Devotees, alone, in groups, or in family groups, eat vanilla, mango, or orange ice cream.

The kiosk located near the Western canteen, where fresh apple juice is sold, looks like a beacon in a sea of sand.

The street on the other side of the Poornachandra is also lit up by the row of stores. Day to day, there are more things for sale in the ashram: drugstore articles, perfumes, bedding, saris, shawls, fruits and vegetables, incense and incense burners, bhajan cassettes, Baba's photos, stationery, and lastly, a place where one can purchase cheese, peanuts, rice, crackers, beverages.

"Swami is offering us more and more comfort," commented the Hindu in charge of selling slippers.

"Swami does not wish devotees to leave the ashram," he tells me and adds with a smile, "and He is accomplishing it!"

Notes taken during the meeting of the Spanish-speaking devotees with Mr. V. K. Narasimhan, present editor of the magazine *Sanathana Sarathi*, on March 9, 1991 in the Central Office of Prasanthi Nilayam.

"Argentina is quite a large country, and so is India." Mr. V. K. Narasimhan mentions the surface of both countries in square miles. He then continues: "Nevertheless, the difference in population between these two countries is enormous: nine hundred million in India, and a little more than thirty million in Argentina. The population of a few cities of India can match the entire population of Argentina.

"Brazil is also large, but it is Portugese. You are Hispanic," translates Bettina through the microphone. Mr. Narasimhan waits for her to finish before continuing: "People come from many different parts of the world, and Swami is very happy with this. They come to India in search of a little village, Puttaparthi. What makes them come here? Why are they attracted? They come because divinity is here in human form."

The voice of Mariana Kenig joins the voice of Bettina Gerschenson translating what has been said by the present editor of the *Sanathana Sarathi*, the monthly magazine that has been published for more than thirty years. Mr. Narasimhan speaks English with a jovial, slow accent. We are in the Central Office, the building located at the foot of the hill where the Administration Building has been erected, and where recently the Museum of all Religions has been built. In the large, well-lit room, we face a small desk with microphones. It is 7:30 P.M.

"Bhagavan Sri Sathya Sai Baba is a unique phenomenon in the history of the world; there has never been anyone like Him in the history of the human race. He was born in a very humble family, in a poor and underdeveloped village. You can see now what happened to this place." He pauses and looks at us.

Everyone's mind is reviewing what we all know of Baba's work in the last fifty years: The busy streets of Puttparthi, the beautiful school buildings at each side of the main avenue, the Planetarium, the magnificent sports field, the Hanuman monument, the airport and the new hospital under construction, and the new housing for devotees in the ashram.

Mr. Narasimhan continues: "From His infancy, Baba showed signs of divinity. The books speak of the miracles He performed, even when a small child." Mr. Narasimhan paused for an instant as if meditating. "He still continues to perform them," he said, and smiled. Then he narrated an occasion when Swami, blowing over two twigs, materialized a cross and gave it to Dr. John Hislop, author of *My Baba and I* and *Conversations with Sathya Sai Baba*.

He continued, "The most important miracle of Baba's is having all human beings realize that they are divine. We are used to looking at ourselves as powerless, weak, and hopeless. Swami has come to declare, 'God is in you; you are divine.' He says this in an indisputable manner. Christ affirmed: 'The kingdom of God is within you,' and added that, once we find the kingdom of heaven, all else will be added unto us. Baba says: 'Realize that you are divine, and then you will experience an unimaginable happiness, which in Sanskrit is known as ananda (bliss).'

"True, in order to experience it," he continued, "it is necessary, as Swami points out, to possess two things: Prema and vairagya, divine love and detachment. This is the opposite of what is happening now. Man's heart is full of hatred and attachment, which is leading a great portion of humanity to the inevitable result: misery. Baba teaches love without egoism. If you have that love, divinity blooms. Swami says: 'Love is God.' I say to you: 'Baba is love.'"

I lift my eyes from the notebook and look around me. I see many familiar faces. Each in his own way has had evidence that Baba is love. I remember my friend Rolo who used to stay late in the canteen collecting the trays from the dinner after all of us had left. His face now shows a radiance resulting from the interview he had this very afternoon with Baba.

"When we come here, we must search for the essence of Swami's teachings. This essence tells us that the Lord resides inside each one of us. There is no need for external Masters. The Master is within us. It is the conscience, the spirit, the higher self. Swami says that we err because we do not obey the voice of our conscience. He says that purity is the road to divinity. Christ said something very beautiful, 'Blessed are the pure in heart because they shall know God.'"

I think of all the devotees of Baba and friends with whom we share this exceptional adventure of coming near and catching a glimpse of the profound mystery of this divine incarnation, Swami, the avatar.

"Baba affirms that purity must be applied not only to the body, but also to the mind, to the heart, and to the way we speak. This is essential in order for us to develop as divine beings. Purity leads us to realize with total certainty that divinity is within us.

"'Use your time here to think of God,' that is what Swami asks of us. 'Do not use your time to go out shopping.'" Then Narasimhan added with a smile, "we can purchase something." He tells us that once when he was outside of India, he "bought an album as a souvenir, containing flowers from the holy land, which were pasted on each page. We can buy something that is of interest to us, but the most important thing is Swami's teachings of love and detachment. Baba's gift is to have us change our attitude every day toward our fellow beings and toward God."

Later on, Mr. Narasimhan told us, "Swami's great miracle is the work that you can see at the canteen. Sometimes they feed three hundred people, and if another five hundred arrive without previous notice, in a minute a meal is prepared for everyone. That is the grace of the Lord."

He asks us to read Baba's books while we are here. "There are some in Spanish," he says. At that moment, pointing to Alberto Vasconcelos, he says, smiling, "You sing very well," and adds, "Swami considers the Argentineans as possessing a high musical level."

Once again, I look around me and remember some voices: the ones of Ruth and Horacio, so much in tune while singing bhajans in duet; the voice of Matias, the two-and-a-half-year-old child who amazed the devotees on the darshan line by singing bhajans after Baba had passed by.

Mr. Narasimhan continues: "Swami has a great love for the people of South America. When Dr. Goldstein informed him of the progress of the Sai Organization in some towns of South America,

Baba was very happy. The Lord says that there will be a great change in the countries of that region and asks that, when you return home, you speak about what you have learned during your stay at Prasanthi Nilayam. This will generate more harmony, more mutual help, and more compassion. We must put all His teaching into practice in our daily lives.

"In this century of hatred and divisiveness, Swami has come to change the consciousness of man and propel him toward a superior level. He has come in order for us to realize that we are a part of God."

Referring to the dissemination of Baba's message, Mr. Narasimhan said, "In this epoch of major advances in science and technology, you can reach any part of the world in a short period of time. When something happens in Australia, it is known in India almost simultaneously. One day," he said with emotion, "a darshan in Puttaparthi will be seen by the entire world. We shall see the Sai revolution in action."

"We are very fortunate. Hundreds of people saw Jesus Christ in a small area in Palestine. They were mainly fishermen and craftsmen. What is happening now? Hundreds of thousands are coming here, and they are physicians, teachers, professionals, and industrialists. Swami's message is not for a small group of individuals, or for one country, but for the entire world. We are the seed of a new international charity. That is how we must consider ourselves. People come from different countries. We see an Australian next to a Guatemalan united in brotherhood. We must create a new world. This is a great opportunity that Baba is offering us."

Later, Mr. Narasimhan asked for questions. Adriana asked him to provide a brief synthesis of what the Sai Organization is doing in India. The editor of the *Sanathana Sarathi* responded: "It is just the same as is happening worldwide. The functions of the Sai Organization are performed by groups in charge of service, education, and devotion. In the first case, the work is performed through medical help and aid to areas where catastrophes have occurred. The service program also provides food and teaches hygiene to the needy."

"The education program is channeled through schools, colleges, and the bal vikas (spiritual education) program. As to the devotional area, the objectives are brought into fruition through the bhajan groups, the celebration of national festivities, and Christmas."

A devotee asked about a particular book about Baba. Mr. Narasimhan responded: "It seems that Swami does not like that book, because the man who published it is profiting from it. I myself have little faith in those writings." (The book alluded to certain prophecies regarding the life of Baba.) He then added: "Why worry about what others say of Swami, if we have Him here?"

Devotee: "What is the actual circulation of the *Sanathana Sarathi* magazine?"

Narasimhan: "The circulation in India is about one hundred thousand. It is edited in eleven languages."

Devotee: "For Swami, does the word 'liberation' mean the same as 'self-realization'? Can one achieve liberation and go on living?"

Narasimhan: "Yes, there are beings who are one with God. This does not mean that they go around creating things. They dedicate their lives to God and live totally devoid of egoism. They consecrate their lives to being joyful and giving themselves entirely to God. Swami says that a good man is God; therefore we must ask ourselves if we are good. These realized beings are those who have no hate. It should be simple for us to be human and to be God. Our problem is we think the Lord is far away from us. Mother Teresa of Calcutta is an example of a person who realizes love without egoism.

"You must develop what the *Bhagavad Gita* propounds in the twelfth chapter in the seventh sloka. This reference asks, who is the devotee that is loved by the Lord? Swami speaks of this, of the signs that point to a good devotee. They are the absence of hate, being friendly toward everyone, being compassionate, helping those who suffer, and being free of possessiveness. He emphasizes being free of 'me' and 'mine.' It is also absence of pride, vanity, and ego, as well as having equanimity in the face of pain and pleasure, the capacity to forgive, being happy, with the mind always focused on God. Man must have the determination to live this life with a spiritual purpose, with his will and intelligence totally dedicated to

God. A devotee like this is loved by the Lord. Only when we think of Him all the time can we leave aside worldly desires. Swami is with us all the time. God is in everything that happens. He is the witness. That is why we must guard against ambition and bad thoughts."

Devotee: "Does the mind need to be destroyed or strengthened in order to be an instrument for realization?"

Narasimhan: "Swami speaks of the mind in two ways; sometimes it ties us and sometimes it liberates us, but we must not think of destroying it. No. We must draw it inward, toward God. Baba says this is simple. Liberation is the ideal state of mind."

Devotee: "Some devotees touch Swami, others cannot do so. Has this anything to do with the type of energy?"

Narasimhan: "Many devotees are anxious to touch Baba, and at that moment and in that manner leave their lives. They are older persons who desire to die like this. But Swami has other reasons for not allowing Himself to be touched by some devotees. Once he stopped a woman from touching Him because the energy emanating from His divine body was so strong that it would have killed her. If the person who is trying to touch Him has an impure mind, Baba will not allow them to do so. Swami wishes that the spiritual energy that passes from Him to us will be received, but we must merit this.

A Spanish devotee who arrived yesterday at the ashram asked about a phenomenon that he and his wife had witnessed while staying at a hotel in Bangalore. They observed strange images forming on the wall. One was a distinct image of Baba. "Is this an illusion, a mirage, or what?" asked the devotee.

Mr. Narasimhan responded: "It is Swami's way to demonstrate that all the gods are one. If you saw the face of Swami, it was real, because He said, 'Anytime you see Me, I am there.'"

Contact with God

"Do not leave Me if I do not look at you. Do not be angry with me. A plant menaced by a pest must be treated. If you feel

124

sorry for the plant but do not apply the necessary medicine because you think the smell is disagreeable, you are not doing the plant any good.

"It would be very easy for Me to make you happy, but what good would that do? After a few years you would realize that the Lord has not helped you very much, for you would have not grown at all. You ask why I cannot make you grow by caressing and stroking you. It is because you would cease to inquire. You would not question yourself about your conduct. You would not seek to discover your defects in order to eliminate them. Nor would you try to change and become better so as to make your Father happy and obtain the gifts He has to give. Surrender to sadness as well as to happiness; they are signs that the Lord has not abandoned you."

The Path

"Beloved Baba, why must we tread such a long road before realizing that all is God?"

"It is for your safety. Listen well: To realize that all is God is completely to transcend the concept of separateness, duality, and pairs of opposites. If the devotees were to reach this level too quickly and too easily, their conduct could be dangerous to themselves and humanity."

"Why, Swami?"

"Because, for a devotee who has realized all is God, what he eats, says, or does would no longer have any importance. All would be—as it is—written by divinity. However, if his conduct is not based on the highest sense of duty, of dharma, if the devotee has not achieved complete detachment, or if his discernment is not complete and perfect, if his love is not free from egoism and able to withstand any test, he could perform many atrocities feeling that God is in each mistaken deed. Because of the lack of his spiritual growth, he would feel that his actions were legitimate.

"Reflecting that the Lord is everything, some devotees act with temerity and abandon, thinking that anything should be permitted because it comes from God. This is not so. God is impeccable, and those who realize Him in each atom of creation must also act impeccably, without error or fault.

"It is unimportant if the devotees think that Swami is unjust for not granting grace equally to everyone. The Lord knows when a devotee is ready to receive the extraordinary gift of realizing that divinity is in everything. He will not permit it to happen before they are ready.

"That is why you are given this road with all its difficulties, so that you may reach perfection and, through it, associate with God. In this way, through your personal experience, you develop the understanding that He is All, including yourself. In my work there are no inconsistencies, no senseless steps. Everything has a secret and powerful reason, which underlies the teachings I expound."

Self-Image

"You have just met with someone who greeted you coldly, with little or no enthusiasm. You say to yourself that this person does not appreciate you. You then decide that this person does not know you, or your circumstances. You try to figure out how to let him know about you because, deep in your heart, you suffer because of this indifference or rejection. You are anxious to be well thought of and accepted.

"You are wasting time. You are rejected or accepted for reasons that are seldom related to you. Either you are their mirror or they are just not interested in you. They are too interested in their own lives, and have no interest in yours.

"How much energy is lost in building images, opinions, and concepts! Let go of them, they are part of your past. Now you have God as your model. It is His opinion that should interest you. It is His concept of you that has value. You must earn His appreciation.

"The Lord knows His devotees, and He evaluates them fairly. In His judgment there are no errors or prejudices. His judgment does not respond to human reasoning or conditions. The Lord knows you. Do not seek beyond Him for acceptance or love from other people. What can compare to the love of the Lord? What love can be more lasting, or more profound? If you have the certainty of the love of the Supreme, how could any adverse human opinion hurt you? You must give love, especially to those who hurt you, ignore you, or despise you. Bathe them in the light that the Lord grants you, and then detach and surrender your life and aspirations to Me. Attach yourself to Me. Take more of My light, My energy, My love, and with them heal the wounds that are caused by the lack of affection from others. Only the love of God is absolute, and He is the only one you must pursue and secure."

Swami's Teachings

"Swami, why is everything so complicated when we try to understand it by ourselves, and so simple when You explain it?"

"Because I impart truth, and truth is simple. The more truthful the knowledge, the closer it is to God, who is the simplest. Certain concepts of the spiritual life may be difficult to understand. This is because of the human thinking process, which becomes aware only after a series of reflections about previous information, experiences, choices, as well as other aspects. All these mental processes interfere with the direct comprehension of spiritual truths. I come and clarify the point; I teach you the ultimate truth, which is a synthesis of what you wish to know.

"The human thinking process is very complex. It does not offer a direct route to achieve your spiritual objective. You may comprehend the objective, but it will always be from a subjective point of view.

"Your Master does not color the essence of the object with His personal viewpoint; He shows it to you just as it is. You call that 'simplicity,' but its true name is wisdom."

Saved

"You are always protected. Swami's robe covers all with His might and His grace. In any circumstance, a devotee knows that he can act from My very being and obtain from Me, just by claiming it, all My divine strength, wisdom, virtue, and truth."

God is Simplicity

"Baba, why is it said that God is simplicity?"

"Because in Him there are no parts. If there were aspects or parts in the being of the Lord, some different from others, there would be no unity in Him."

"Is it saying that God is formed by just one element, Swami?"

"Not by 'one' element, but by 'the' one universal element."

"Which one, Baba?"

"The divinity that is the essence of God."

"Lord, could we ever conceive this essence of God in all its fullness?"

"Never."

God's Love (II)

"When you say 'Baba does not love me," you are comparing this meeting with Me with some experience you had with another person who did not love you. You believe that

God's love is manifested in a prescribed manner, and you assign a measure to My conduct in order to evaluate what I give you.

"God's love cannot be measured through human standards. Human love is possessive, egoistic, changeable, conditioned, and vulnerable. God does not love you as you love others. God loves you better. God loves you perfectly.

"The Lord does not want to possess you. The Lord wants you to possess Him completely. He wants you to totally incorporate Him into your life. He wants you to develop the gifts He grants you without delay or hesitation. God is anxious for you to learn to love your brothers in His way, which is unconditional and liberating. Above all, love yourself, discarding those limiting ideas about your own circumstances.

"I cannot give you the complete demonstration of My love, for you would die if you experienced it. Such is the power of my gift, such is the depth of my sentiment, such is the magnitude of My energy. Your being could not remain an instant in this world if I were to show it to you in its fullness. That is why I let you glimpse it through a look or a gesture of Mine, a teaching, a gift. That is why I give you only a glimpse of the magnificence of My divine love that never abandons, hurts, or confuses, and that asks only for an open heart to tirelessly give itself.

"That is why when you say 'Swami does not love me,' I smile and greet you as a little child who has lost his way and still does not know where peace resides. There is still to be born in him the certainty of My living presence, faithful and strong. I say to you today, "Do not compare Me with anyone whom you have known before. God is beyond comparison."

Lust

"Baba, could you please explain to me why lust is as destructive as the other enemies of man on the spiritual path, such as anger and envy?"

"Because lust is an excess, an excess of the senses that

129

chains man to one of the lowest expressions of his identity. Observe that I say 'the lowest' in a strictly functional sense; I am referring to the anatomical structure of man's brain that commands the sensations, which existed way before the development of his higher intellect. This is the part of the brain where man acquires capacities that differentiate him from animals.

"Lust directs man to search for pleasure, which is always egoistic, and exacerbates the search, which is fruitless. At the end of the cycle, he finds himself at the same point where he started. There will have been no change, just a momentary satisfaction."

"Why did you say that it is an egoistic pleasure, Swami?"

"The nature of his body drives man to obtain natural pleasure in the human encounter. When a couple unites in marriage, the deep affection will be expressed in their ability to give and receive, and permit them to transcend the purely biological act. If there are children from this union, it will seal with the power of creation the sacredness of the bond.

"Love is generosity, altruism, and giving; lust is self-serving. The object of lust once obtained is discarded. Moreover, it is scorned, as you reject an exquisite dish that is offered to you when your appetite has been appeased. Before eating, food seems appetizing to you, but after a very abundant meal, what initially was desired is now rejected. There is no generosity in lust. Man thinks only of himself and his body. That is all."

"How does one become lustful, Lord?"

"The same way one becomes gluttonous. It is due to lack of control. If you accustom your stomach to receive a great quantity of sweets, it will ask you for more and more sweets. The stomach has a stimulus and response mechanism. You only need to wait for your stomach to be empty for the desire to eat to return. That is why there is no real satisfaction, because it is neither lasting nor cumulative. You alternate between being surfeited and empty. In neither of those two extremes is there pleasure, and neither assures the elimination of the other. It is a vicious circle where you find yourself over and over at the starting point. This is where obsession begins."

"Obsession, Baba?"

"Man desires peace, but between desire and satisfaction there is conflict. In that conflict there is no growth. However, you can never get too much spiritual food. The pleasures of the spirit are permanent and expansive. The more growth, the more freedom is achieved. The pleasures of the body always leave man unsatisfied. He becomes obsessed, wanting the reward that he never got. What he does get is temporary fullness. You may say that he enjoys himself as long as he eats, but once the appetite is satisfied, that is to say, overly satisfied (we have said that lust is an excess), then rejection occurs, and in that rejection of the object, which was so desired, lies the seed of self-deprecation. For man knows that after awhile he will again desire what now appears disagreeable to him. This is the worst kind of attachment."

"Why is it the worst kind, Swami?"

"Have you ever heard that spiritual growth makes man perverted, makes him act contrary to his moral duty, and makes him totally aggressive? No. But, the man who is attached to the pleasure of the senses nurtures the animal part that is in him, and ends up by not being in charge of his own emotions or actions. The organic functions of the body do not have a code of conduct. If they dominate, man moves away from his transcendent spiritual identity."

"Because of his questionable values, Swami?"

131

"Because of his mishandling of his energy. You know that there is only one kind of energy. There are no diverse types; there are only the different manifestations of the one energy. The lack of control over the senses drives one to waste energy, so that he can never go beyond the limits of the biological plane. That is why this is a very difficult trap to escape."

"Lord, how can it be explained that certain teachings recommend the use of sensuality in order to reach illumination.?"

"There is only one answer: ignorance. Ignorance about what man is, what he can really achieve through the use of the body, and ignorance of the meaning of illumination. In order to grow spiritually, self-knowledge is essential. This is possible only through relentless clarity and self-control, which will ensure that the direction of the flow of energy is toward the one goal, the direct experience of the transcendent divine consciousness. Those experiences where man loses his identity in some physical activity have never provided him with any growth and cannot be farther away from samadhi, the highest degree of the expansion of consciousness.

"Pretending that both things are the same, or proposing that sensuality is the road to God, is as mistaken as affirming that learning to control the breath in a certain way will bring you to the Supreme. Only love without egoism, detachment, self-control, and surrender to the highest can lead man to the divine kingdom. Do not doubt this. Lust is a gift that is deceiving. It seduces you with the promise of pleasure, which disappears like mist. And what are you left with? Fatigue and depression, and the wait for another attack of desire. In the meantime, have you grown? Do you know yourself better? Because you have satisfied your senses, would you be more capable of working for the improvement of the world tomorrow? Can you save up your experiences or advance with your work from such ephemeral desires? This kind of fulfillment only gives you temporary self-forgetfulness, but you remain

132

the same at the beginning and at the end. Nothing has changed in your interior, nor are you better prepared for love, which is what really matters."

"Baba, is lust a vice?"

"Lust is an error. The search for love is legitimate, but the chosen path is a mistaken one. Everyone wishes for the best. God attracts His children toward His bosom, and this is perceived by the divine spark nestled within each heart. Some, hearing the call, believe it comes from the world. They get lost in the moving sands of the senses. Others dive into sensuousness in order to deafen the divine voice, because to listen to it would perhaps require them to reject the senseless way in which their lives are spent. So they choose not to know, not to fight, not to believe, and they try to get rid of their anguish in the illusion of life, which offers them some momentary forgetfulness. Lack of control helps man to escape from himself. Self-control, on the other hand, demands that he have an acute awareness of himself.

"Fear alienates, gluttony makes you into an animal, anger takes you out of your center, envy poisons, jealousy denigrates, lust subjugates. They are all implacable patterns that have a common denominator: bondage.

"It is important for you to know that no one can enslave you. To realize freedom is an inner victory. Bondage is self-inflicted. You can be limited by things outside of yourself. They can confine, shackle, or even kill you. But, if your character has been forged in the crucible of the soul, there would be no power in the world that could enslave you. It is your own choice that enslaves you. Likewise, it is your own choice that liberates you.

"I am here to guide you, to help you come to Me, to return you to that secret place in the depth of your hearts where I call each of you. Give me your life, I will remove all difficulties, and I will provide you with the cure for every ailment. No one can understand your problems like Swami. No one accepts you as I do.

"The goal of the spiritual path is bliss. Dedicate your efforts to achieve this. Use your body as a precious instrument to reach God. Always aspire to the highest. The achievement of true happiness is not by chance, it is your right and you should not give it up."

Testimony

Something very strange, beautiful, and full of significance has just happened. More than two weeks ago, I placed four decorative stones behind some books on a shelf in my library. There were some chimes hanging under it. Today I was in my room meditating. I was visualizing the light of Baba illuminating the world when impulsively I asked, "Baba! Are You here?" Immediately the chimes sounded with a strong and prolonged vibration. I opened my eyes and saw them oscillating from the impact of one of the four decorative stones. Without the intervention of any apparent force, the stone separated from the others, fell off the shelf, and crashed against the metal chimes. The stone was now resting on a chair.

I murmured for a long time, "Baba, Baba, Baba!" while the echoes of the chimes vibrated inside me.

Then reasoning intervened. I measured, calculated, and evaluated the inexplicable, knowing in my innermost self that the only explanation was that this was Swami's response to my question: "Baba! Are You here?"

Then I received this message:

"God's manifestations are infinite. Man looks at them with the scrutiny of reason and seeks an explanation that will answer the profound question about the truth of divine omnipresence. But man cannot understand divinity. He must accept, that is all. He must offer his faith and open his heart to the flow of love of the Lord, who only wants to give His children the sweet awareness of Himself in their lives.

"Do not shield yourself from the Lord's divine intervention

134

in your affairs. Do not reject His mysterious incarnation with your rational thought and your lack of understanding. Do not deny Him a space in your innermost being. Do not deny Him the opportunity of bathing you in the warmth of His love. When His love manifests, it is for you to enjoy the richness of that other dimension toward which He is calling you.

"Each time you call Me, I manifest Myself. Each time I am named, I give the devotee evidence of My nearness. Sometimes it is through a feeling, a wave of peace or of happiness. Other times I manifest through an idea where a long-awaited answer reaches you. Sometimes I show Myself through a sound that is produced without explanation, a photograph that falls, a perfume that seems to come from nowhere. Or simply, I flood your hearts with joy because you are My devotees and I love you."

Why Man is Born

"Baba, why is man born?"

"To realize God."

"Swami, please explain further."

"The seed does not know that it has a tree inside it. Nor is it aware that it has flowers and fruits that are in perfect communion with the roots and soil. It does not know that it has in it the potential to sprout and move its branches toward the sun. The seed does not know that there is abundant food as sap circulating in its tree, nor does it know that it will be reborn each spring. The seed does not know about the winds that will caress it, or the birds that will nest in its branches. In the same way, man cannot imagine the glory of his destiny. Man seeks with his limited mind for a reason to justify his life and his encounter with God.

"With your present feelings, emotions, and thoughts, you do not have anything that is in any way comparable with the

135

experience that awaits you. That is why you are told to surrender, to love, to trust, so that you can grow into that moment where there will be no more questions, only certainty, happiness, and indescribable bliss. Why does God gives you this? His only reason is love."

EPILOGUE

Baba's Message to Me

"The nature of God is incomprehensible and mysterious. He is the indweller in each of you, and He is the moving force of each action you engage in. He is both the act itself and the power that generates it. He is the cause, the effect, and the energy that emerges out of that relationship. Because He is the Source of life, all His manifestations belong to Him. God is the inborn and immanent. He is the eternal stillness and the movement that emerges from it. He generates change and remains changeless. The Lord is the omnipresent, the one who accompanies you and is never absent. Words such as 'always' and 'never,' which are opposite to each other, are not appropriate when used in describing divinity, because in eternity everything happens simultaneously, and, therefore, the Lord is beyond the duality of the pairs of opposites.

"God is innate in creation and exists in every manifestation.

"Omnipresence is not only the essence of each object but also the conscience of each being. Omnipresence fully exists in every manifested form and cannot be separated from the undifferentiated and mysterious One.

"God is not only the witness, He is the experience itself. He is the theater and the play. He is the feelings and the most intimate thoughts of each actor in the human drama. I do not say to My devotees, 'I was there. I saw you and, therefore, I know what happened to you.' Rather I say, 'I was the place. I was the seer and that which was seen.

"I am every level of consciousness. I am the pure state of knowledge. I am the substance that is beyond the known and beyond memory.

"You say: 'Swami is here,' and announce Me as a third person, without realizing that I am the One constantly in each one of you.

"The Lord, omnipresent by the will of His infinite power, is

137

the manifestation that He Himself has created, and at the same time He is the contemplator of His manifestation and also its Master.

"God truly is the great mystery, and you are given the opportunity to contemplate Him in the one aspect that is closest to human understanding: the divine incarnation. His attributes are identical to the attributes of the Supreme. Baba is here on this earth for the benefit of all of humanity.

"Now I tell My devotees: The divine omnipresence is the immediate boon that I reserve for all. Each one may experience this grace as his own by opening the door that leads from disbelief into the hall of faith, where My promise is fulfilled. The key to opening that door is surrender. When surrender is without reservation, the gift of God is infinite."

Sathya Sai Baba Books from Leela Press

A Catholic Priest Meets Sai Baba by Don Mario Mazzoleni. The theologian discovers through much study and doubt that Sai Baba is a Divine Incarnation. 285 pages, $12.00

The Dharmic Challenge (*Putting Sathya Sai Baba's Teachings into Practice*) compiled and edited by Judy Warner. A provocative collection of stories that illustrate the joys and difficulties of living a dharmic life. 181 pages, $11.00.

The Dreams & Realities, Face to Face with God by Dr. Naresh Bhatia. The author's devotion to God illuminates the pages of this spiritual autobiography. As head of the blood bank of Sai Baba's Super Specialty Hospital, Bhatia experiences frequent contacts, unique opportunities, and wondrous miracles with Sai Baba. 192 pages, $12.00

Journey to Sathya Sai Baba (*A Visitor's Guide*) by Valmai Worthington. A primer for first time travelers to Sai Baba's ashram. $86 pages, $7.00.

Pathways to God by Jonathan Roof. 27 topics that give a clear and accurate guide to the teachings of Sathya Sai Baba. 211 pages, $12.00.

Sai Baba's Mahavakya on Leadership by Lieut Gen (Retd) Dr. M. L. Chibber. A step-by-step program on how to build character and reestablish leadership inspired by idealism. 212 pages, $12.00.

Sai Inner Views and Insights by Howard Murphet. Another Murphet triumph tracing Murphet's life with Sai Baba over the last 30 years. He not only describes miracles vividly, but shares his experiences and insights into Sai Baba's teachings. 184 pages, $12.00.

Song of My Life (*A Journey to the Feet of Sathya Sai Baba*) by Jeannette Caruth. The author tells the story of her transformation in fluent poetry which occasionally rises to the height of spiritual revelation. 118 pages, $9.00.

Where the Road Ends by Howard Murphet. The author's odyssey in search of the meaning of his life from childhood to old age. The book shows how Baba brings a deeper understanding of life's purpose. 209 pages, $12.00

If unavailable at your bookstore, call Leela Press (804) 361-1132.